ACKNOWLEDGMENTS

Networlding is a collaboration of dedicated thought leaders across the country and the world that:

- Share in the belief that anything is possible,
- Strive to make a positive difference in the lives of others, and
- Do good while doing well.

Networlding is the art and science of making meaningful connections and leveraging those connections in new and powerful ways. Our best practices are designed to help your organization master the intersection of traditional networking and social media.

Our proven content will allow your best assets – your people – to learn the Networlding process, creating and leveraging anetwork of support for both short term and long term goals – ultimately transforming your business.

The creation of this training course is an example of Networlding in action: Values, Collaboration and Leadership. I would like to acknowledge and thank the following people from the Networlding leadership team for their dedication, service, and excellence:

Amy Franko, Instructional Designer and Networlding Facilitator, based in Columbus, OH. Amy provided the instructional design direction for this course, and was instrumental in the creation of both the facilitator and participant guides.

Doreen Nicastro, Social Media Strategist and Networlding Facilitator, based in Boston, MA. Doreen provided essential project management support, editing, and overall coordination.

Andrew Curtis, President, Fuel VM, based in Indianapolis, IN. Andrew provided the artistic eye and visual direction, plus cover design and internal artwork.

My sincere hope that your organization finds value in this course, and applies its principles for the greatest success. It is in true alignment with the mission of Networlding, "creating the greatest good for the greatest number."

Melissa Giovagnoli,
Founder and CEO, Networlding
www.networlding.com

TABLE OF CONTENTS

LEGEND

Each step contains an agenda, objectives, lessons, and exercises. There are several instructional cues in this guide to help you lead a Networlding course.

SCRIPT: Each step contains scripts to help you guide the class. As you become more familiar with the content, you may want to your own scripts. Scripts cover key concepts, and help with the course flow.

FACILITATOR NOTE: Facilitator notes contain additional support for content, activities, and class management. Be sure to familiarize yourself with them.

DIRECTIONS FOR FACILITATOR: Each exercise contains facilitator directions to help with proper setup and delivery.

DEBRIEF: Exercises and discussions contain a debrief, helping you guide the class uncover conclusions and better apply the content.

CLOSING DISCUSSION: This will allow you to conclude a step and properly setup the next Networlding step.

INTRODUCTION TO NETWORLDING

The Facilitator Guide is designed as a resource to help you facilitate groups through the seven steps of the Networlding methodology. To support your work, you will find suggested timelines, scripts, notes, activities, and dialogue points along the way. You are welcome to tailor these as you see fit to create the best experience for your audience or circle group.

For this segment, you may want a flip chart or whiteboard. Participants have a corresponding guide to follow along. Take time to familiarize yourself with the participant guide.

AGENDA

Customize the agenda timing as needed. You may want to combine the Introduction and Step 1.

TIME	ACTION	OBJECTIVE
10 minutes	Welcome and Logistics	Communicate objectives
10 minutes	Icebreaker	Establish early rapport; demonstrates Emotional Exchange Model
30 – 40 minutes	**Lesson 1**: Networking vs. Networlding – Why Does It Matter?	Elicit group perspectives
20 minutes	**Lesson 2**: What Is Your Networlding IQ?	Learn place on Networlding continuum

OBJECTIVES

The objectives for the Introduction:

- Compare our understanding of networking and Networlding and why Networlding matters today

- Understand our Networlding IQ, and what we can do to improve our Networlding IQ

- Discover the values that will become our foundation in creating Networlding relationships

Net(worlding

VALUES. COLLABORATION. LEADERSHIP.

WELCOME AND LOGISTICS (10 MINUTES)

Facilitator creates a script to describe the following:

- What Networlding means to him/her
- How he/she came to be there facilitating the course
- Objectives for the overall course and the day's session
- Any pertinent logistical information

The facilitator should be working to:

- Establish rapport with the participants early on
- Create a safe environment for sharing information, ideas, goals, and dreams
- Model Networlding values and the support exchange model

SCRIPT: [The following is a sample. Be sure to create your own.]

Welcome to Networlding! I'm Amy Franko, a Networlding facilitator. It's so exciting for me to be here with you to grow our knowledge on this very relevant topic.

And just to demonstrate the power of building relationships, I'll share with you the path I took to be here today. It all started with a request I made to Melissa via LinkedIn, asking for her LinkedIn tips guide. Melissa did some research on my profile, and saw the possibilities for us in getting to know one another better. She reached out to me and in Networlding style, we were on the phone for quite some time, sharing stories and creating the beginning of the support base that's so necessary for Networlding relationships. As the relationship grew, we ultimately identified some collaboration possibilities, and becoming a Networlding facilitator presented itself.

Networlding to me is how we should move through the world building relationships. So many of us don't like the word "networking" - it carries negative connotations for us, and especially as women. Networlding is a way for us to truly collaborate with those who have the traits we value - for the good of all involved. It's a way for us to use our natural strengths, and be ourselves in the process. And as we move through this process, you'll hopefully develop your own view of Networlding.

So as we move through this session, there are a couple of objectives we are looking to accomplish:

- Compare our understanding of networking and Networlding and why Networlding matters today
- Understand our Networlding IQ, and what we can do to improve our Networlding IQ
- Discover the values that will become our foundation in creating Networlding relationships

There are a couple of important things to keep in mind as we work together:

- Your stories, ideas, and knowledge are important - please know that it's safe to share them in this environment
- We all have many experiences that brought us here today, so let's learn from one another.
- I'm here to facilitate, but not necessarily tell you how to do something. I know I'll learn as much from you as I hope you learn from being here.
- To make the most of this course you need to apply what we learn - it's the only way to retain and improve our knowledge.
- Develop rapport and chemistry first before discussing leads and referrals.
- Be an active listener, listening more than we talk. Learn about the individual first so that you may find ways to support them.

ICEBREAKER (10 MINUTES)

FACILITATOR NOTE: Icebreaker assumes people in class don't know one another. If that's not the case, substitute another icebreaker/activity suitable to the class.

FACILITATOR NOTE: This activity will help establish early rapport. Notice that there are two "phases" to this introduction exercise. In the first phase, the participants are simply sharing some basic facts. In the second phase, they are going a bit deeper and sharing some more personal information and a point of commonality. This second phase demonstrates Emotional Support in the exchange model.

SCRIPT: We're going to get started with some conversation. At your tables, share the following information:

- Introduce yourself (keep it brief)
- One thing you'd like to take away from the workshop

Now add the following information:

- Share one interesting fact about yourself
- Share what always makes you laugh or brings a smile to your face
- Share what you love to do, or would love to do more of in your life
- Once you've done that, as a group identify one thing you all have in common at the table. An example might be that you all have children.

You'll have about 5 minutes to complete the activity before we come back together as a group.

DEBRIEF: In the interest of time, ask two questions:

1. Ask which "phase" of the introduction they related to in a better way.

2. Ask each table to share the one thing they all have in common. Tie icebreaker to Support Exchange Model, emotional support.

SCRIPT: We've gone around the room and shared information and found some commonalities. Those are the beginnings of building Networlding relationships. What you've done is establish the beginnings of the Support Exchange Model. The first piece is emotional support - creating rapport, and mutual trust and affinity.

LESSON 1 - NETWORKING VS. NETWORLDING - WHY DOES IT MATTER? (30-40 MINUTES)

SCRIPT: This brings us to lesson 1, defining networking vs. Networlding - and why it matters. Certainly there is passing resemblance between networking and Networlding - both revolve around the concept of forming relationships. But the resemblance ends once you understand the traits of Networlding.

I'd like to start by getting your views.

- What traits come to mind when you think of networking?
- What traits come to mind when you think of Networlding?

FACILITATOR NOTE: List answers on a flipchart. Once their knowledge and understanding level have been captured, add some of these additional traits to the conversation. Ask participants to share a couple of stories where they have seen either networking or Networlding in action, and what they learned from it.

Traits of Networking	Traits of Networlding
Temporary	Long-term commitment
Goal-based	Values-based
Duplication of efforts	Leveraged learning
Many times one-sided	Mutually beneficial
Transactional	Relational
Haphazard process	Conscious, strategic process
Fragmented	Systematic
Materialistic	Holistic
Superficial	Intimate
Opportunity specific	Opportunity expansive
Two-dimensional	Multi-dimensional

DEBRIEF: Moving forward, here are some important key points to remember. There is space in your guide for you to take notes.

In **networking:**

- Connections are often flimsy because they lack ongoing support
- People are bound together because one person needs the other for a project, sale, or deal. It's often one-sided.
- One particular situation binds the two together - and once that situation ends, the relationship isn't strong enough to sustain itself.

In **Networlding:**

- Relationships begin when you're clear in your intent - in the broad sense of the word.
- You communicate your goals and values, and those who resonate with that will respond to you.
- When someone responds positively, and you're able to establish a Networlding relationship, both can reap the benefits.
- This new partner, or potential new partner, will become a source of fresh ideas, support, and help bring about more opportunities.

FACILITATOR NOTE: Ask the participants to provide a few reasons why Networlding matters, and why it's far more effective than networking. Once they have shared their personal examples, continue with the following:

SCRIPT: **First,** The Networlding Way is a strategic method to stay connected to ever changing resources, exchange and grow opportunities, and to strengthen and build transformational relationships.

The Networlding Way uses the Science of Networks along with the advantages of Social Media and today's technology to provide the ability to make a difference in an energized and expansive ways not possible by just networking.

The Networlding 7 step process has built its foundation on the following values:

- Making a difference
- Innovation
- Collaboration
- Integrity

Relationships that develop from Networlding are connected beyond a task, have shifted from me to WE, have communication that includes clear articulation and focused listening, vision and diversity.

Second, the Networlding Way is a new way of creating meaningful relationships.

Things in our fast paced world are constantly changing; we need to stay closely connected through our relationships. Others are receiving a constant flow of information just like you, and with their different perspectives could offer information of value to us that may have been outside of our awareness.

In Networlding, we organize our relationships in three different types: primary, secondary, and tertiary. We'll cover those types more in depth in step 2.

To help determine what connection goes into which group, look at:

- Values shared
- Frequency of contact
- Overlapping goals
- Availability
- Level of exchange and
- Type of exchange or opportunity

Third, the Networlding Way uses the Support Exchange model, which you were just briefly introduced to in the icebreaker exercise and will learn more about in step 4. This model follows the natural progression of meaningful relationships.

The model follows 7 steps - what you just saw in the icebreaker were the first two: emotional support and informational support. As we grow a relationship, we begin to share at a deeper level and create transformational opportunities over time.

The top level is creating community, or a ripple effect from multiple exchanges. And you'll notice the entire model is surrounded by fulfillment - which is ultimately what we are looking for ourselves, and looking to help others create.

Networlding Support Exchange Model

LESSON 2 - WHAT IS YOUR NETWORLDING IQ? (20 MINUTES)

SCRIPT: Are we Networlders? Some of us naturally practice Networlding, but know that it is something that can be learned - it's a skill. Each of us is unique, and we're all somewhere on the Networlding continuum. So how do we know if we're pursing relationships and opportunities in a purposeful way?

We'll start with a self assessment to know where we are on the continuum. This self-assessment is based on beliefs, strategies, and behaviors of those who are already consciously practicing Networlding. Read each question and rate how often you practice these behaviors.

There are no right or wrong answers - you won't be graded, so answer them honestly and don't over think it! Let's take about 10 minutes to complete.

Questions	Never 1	Seldom 2	Occasionally 3	Often 4	Always 5
Share your goals with others					
Build/nurture relationships with those who can help you achieve your goals					
Limit relationships with selfish individuals and those that don't help you realize your goals					
Respect the creative process and are result/outcome focused					
Believe that Networking/Networlding shortens the time to get things done					
Assume that Networking/Networlding is a balanced process of giving and receiving					
Believe Networking/Networlding can provide all needed resources to reach your goals					

Questions	Never 1	Seldom 2	Occasionally 3	Often 4	Always 5
When Networking/Networlding you ask for what you want					
When Networking/Networlding you discover others' interests and needs					
When Networking/Networlding you expect to discover/create new opportunities					
Network/Networld with influential people who can make things happen					
Offer emotional, information and other support to your Network/Networld partners					
Respond quickly to the requests and needs of your Network/Networld partners					
Measure the results of your Networking/Networlding efforts					
Believe it is important to make a difference					
Believe that anything is possible					
Believe you are guided by strong inner beliefs, intent or principles					
Believe you create your own rewards					
Believe you can get anything done through others					
Questions	Never 1	Seldom 2	Occasionally 3	Often 4	Always 5
Believe people are your most creative resource					

TOTAL SCORE: _____

SCRIPT: When you've finished, take a minute to find your place on the Networlding continuum. There are four phases to the continuum.

FACILITATOR NOTE: Briefly touch on the 4 phases. These same descriptions are in the participant guide for them to read and absorb in detail.

Phase	Description
Novice (20-44)	You're an entry-level networker. You've probably established a baseline network of friends, family members, and co-workers. You may participate in professional or community organizations, but typically novices aren't in leadership roles. You may have started to think about values-based relationships, but haven't yet begun sharing your values, goals, and beliefs with others. Some reasons people stay in the novice category can include fear of rejection, or the belief that you don't have enough value to offer. **Despite misgivings you might have about reaching out to others, start by making your goals, values, and beliefs known.**
Networker (45-64)	You are a true networker, likely to have expanded beyond your circle of family, friends, and colleagues to include those from industry associations or community organizations. You recognize influential people and make an effort to meet them. You may even have a large directory of contacts. Despite your ability to meet and greet, you are not generating the relationship quality or opportunities you desire. The contacts you've made don't necessarily represent relationships; you may not follow up on a consistent basis, or if you do establish a surface relationship the trust and shared goals have yet to be developed. **Learn to focus your efforts on developing relationships that are based on valuable exchanges. You'll begin to experience the naturally beneficial opportunities that Networlding provides.**

Strategic Networlder (65-84)	You've moved well beyond traditional networking and entered the realm of Networlding. You most likely target and qualify those with whom you spend your time, share your intent with those in your circle, grow contacts into meaningful relationships, exchange different types of support, schedule meetings and perform regular follow up, and leverage relationships to develop opportunities for yourself and others. **You are instinctively doing the right things. The next step is to broaden your skills into a systematic approach for even greater success.**
Networlding Expert (85-100)	You're a top-level Networlder. You most likely have circles with broad access to people with varied interests and skills, exchange support on all levels, acquire whatever resources you lack through others, interact with influential individuals, establish mutually beneficial opportunities, and form personal strategic alliances. **Refresh, refine, and further extend your Networlding skills and processes to achieve even greater fulfillment.**

DEBRIEF: Ask if anyone is willing to share where they are on the continuum. Ask them to circle any of the questions or statements that really stood out to them as traits they would like to specifically work on.

SCRIPT: So we've learned where we are on the continuum, and remember that Networlding is a set a steps and skills that we practice over time. No matter where you currently are on the continuum, the skills we'll learn here will help us improve or refine what we're currently doing.

There are some fill-in-the-blanks in your participant guide to follow along.

FACILITATOR NOTE: Fill-in-the blanks are underlined in the bullets below.

1. Our goal is NOT to achieve an expert status.
2. Our goals are to improve on the skills, behaviors, and mind-set that Networlding represents. Focus on continuous improvement.

SCRIPT: Let's look at how we can increase our Networlding IQ. There are 5 key actions:

1. **Visualize your Networld.** This is about shifting your frame of reference from a flat, static series of contacts to an evolving, multi-tiered group of connections. Picture yourself in the center of a living organism. The cells surrounding you represent your connections - all people you like and trust. Each cell provides a unique and valuable function. As the organism grows, it changes form, learns new things, and gains experience. Cells are added and replaced to keep the organism functioning as a whole.

Your Networld is something that evolves and changes over time but is always functioning.

2. **Establish connections with bridgers.** Bridgers are those individuals who bring together people from different groups to develop new opportunities. Bridgers can be just about anyone - they're the ones who seem to know everyone, have a knack for anticipating who will work well together, and love to make introductions. Your Networld must have bridgers - they're the link between you and others who can become important Networlding partners.

3. **Create inner and outer circles.** Every well-functioning Networld has an inner circle and a series of outer circles. This helps you to organize your relationships and focus your energy on the right people at the right time. Your primary circle is critical - within the primary circle are those people who most closely align with your values and goals, you have frequent contact and support exchanges. This circle holds anywhere from 3-10 influential people. Your outer circles represent weaker ties, but these people are still valuable.

Those within your outer circles are usually great sources of information, referrals, and ideas. It's impossible to have strong bonds with everyone. So focus on your primary circle first, and then begin creating relationships with influencers.

4. **Identify and include influencers.** People who are influencers use their knowledge, skills, experience, reputation, and resources to make things happen. They aren't always in positions of what we consider to be traditional power. Influence not about force. We've probably experienced someone who is considered powerful to use negative tactics, such as intimidation, to influence an outcome. True influencers affect the opinions and behaviors of others through positive means.

5. **Maximize your connectivity.** Use multiple methods, both online and offline, to create and sustain relationships. In today's world of social networking, it would create a big hole in your Networlding strategy to not use all of the tools available to you. Many connections made initially online evolve into deeper personal relationships. It's important to strike a balance with all your connection methods.

CLOSING DISCUSSION: Ask for any additional questions, comments, or takeaways that the class has uncovered before moving on to step 1. You may also summarize the main points.

STEP 1 – ESTABLISH A VALUES-RICH FOUNDATION

The first step in Networlding is creating a values-rich foundation. This step is about becoming consciously aware of our values and then creating goals and actions that reflect those values.

For this segment, you may want a flip chart or whiteboard. Participants have a corresponding guide to follow along. Take time to familiarize yourself with the participant guide.

AGENDA

Customize the agenda timing as needed.

TIME	ACTION	OBJECTIVE
60 minutes	**Lesson 1**: Creating Your Foundation	Establish values, strengths, goals, and actions
	Exercise 1: Value Priorities	
	Exercise 2: Identify Your Strengths, Goals, & Actions	
20-30 minutes	**Lesson 2**: Networlding Beliefs	Identify the common beliefs Networlders share, and how to look for them

OBJECTIVES

The objectives for Step 1:

- Discover the values that will become our foundation in creating Networlding relationships
- Identify beliefs common among Networlders, and how to look for them in others

14

LESSON 1 – CREATING YOUR FOUNDATION (60 MINUTES)

SCRIPT: Up to this point, we've compared networking to Networlding, discovered our Networlding IQ, and ways to continually improve it.

That brings us to the first step in Networlding - creating a values-rich foundation. This step is about becoming consciously aware of your values and then creating goals that reflect those values. When you stop to think about, we can often fall into the cycle of working with people or on projects that don't align with our values or goals.

Think of your values-rich foundation like a house. There are some key steps to building a house right? Here's a summary of the steps:

1. Identify your value priorities.

2. Identify your strengths.

3. Identify your goals.

4. Create action steps that are aligned with your goals and priorities.

First, let's identify our value priorities. Your values have been established over time, but sometimes we aren't always *aware* of them. When you identify your values, you will begin to see them in those that might make great Networlding partners for you.

Values clarification is also an imperative step in the transition from doing the things you are skilled at to doing the things you are passionate about. You can be competent without being passionate about a job, project or task. **When you identify an overlap between what motivates you and where you excel, you've found a passion!**

If you don't define your values, you risk establishing relationships with people who operate from a valueless base. For example, have you ever done work for someone or entered into a business partnership with someone that didn't feel quite right? Like maybe you were selling out? Chances are good that person didn't operate from the same value base as you.

EXERCISE 1 – VALUE PRIORITIES

FACILITATOR NOTE: allow about 15-20 minutes total for this exercise. This exercise is divided into 3 parts.

SCRIPT: You'll see a list of some value priorities in your guide. This isn't an exhaustive list, so feel free to add your own as you see fit.

All of the values listed are important. You are identifying what drives you. For example, do not feel compelled to select "family" as a value if it is not what motivates you to action. That does not mean you don't care for your family.

We're going to do a short exercise to help us better uncover our values.

Values List			
Achievement	Advancement	Adventure	Affiliation
Authority	Autonomy	Balance	Collaboration
Community	Competence	Competition	Connection
Contribution	Cooperation	Courage	Creativity
Economic prosperity	Economic security	Empowerment	Fame
Family	Focus	Freedom	Friendship
Fun	Giver	Happiness	Health
Helpfulness	Honoring	Inner Harmony	Integrity
Involvement	Knowing	Knowledge	Loyalty
Making a Difference	Non-judgment	Order	Personal Development
Pleasure	Power	Quality	Recognition
Responsibility	Safety	Self Motivation	Self respect
Service	Spirituality	Success	Trust
Wisdom			

FACILITATOR NOTE: Your objectives are the following -

- Begin a dialogue about what the participants believe the word "values" represents. This will also give you an idea of where they are at in their thinking process.

- Get them out of their heads and into where their cores values exist. Ideally you want the participants to experience their values.

- Inform the class that the values list is simply a list of words. We apply the meaning to the value. Values represent a state of being and what's important to us.

16

- Values either bring us to a certain action, or stop us from doing something. They provide internal motivation and guidance. It's the only
path to authenticity and fulfillment. Sometimes when we are focus on external motivators the fulfillment is short lived (think of a shopping spree, a raise, the latest gadget.)

- Participants should become active listeners. Listening is a key skill in the Networlding process.

PART 1 – DIRECTIONS FOR FACILITATOR:

1. If you have a co-facilitator, you will want to demo this with that person. If not, ask for a volunteer from the group.

2. Ask your demo partner to select 1 value of theirs.

3. Then ask the following questions, where (value) changes to the answer of the previous question.

FACILITATOR DEMO SCRIPT: When you are experiencing   (value) ,

1. What do you get from   (value)   ?

2. What does having   (value)   do for you?

3. What is important about   (value)   ?

4. When you have   (value)   , what is even more important than that?

SCRIPT: Now that you have seen this demo, here's what I would like you to do:

1. Create pairs or triads.

2. One of you will take the **explorerrole** (being asked the questions), one of you will be **the guide** (asks the questions and only listens, no interpreting, records words used by explorer to describe).

3. If you have a third person, that role is to observe both the guide and explorer, record words that the explorer expresses, and provide support for the guide if needed.

FACILITATOR NOTE: If it's a large group, triads work well. They should break into threes, and then the facilitator sets up the explorer, guide and observer by perhaps assigning A, B, C to the sets.

SCRIPT: As you are working through this exercise keep these things in mind:

- You could end up with a different value than the one you started with.

- Ask the questions as stated with no embellishment or elaborating.

- Listen as a witness, without interpretation, repeating back exactly as shared, with full focus on what the other person is sharing.

- It does not matter in the end what the value is called, all that matters is that it is clear to the explorer

DEBRIEF: Once they had a few minutes to go through the above exercise, bring them back for a discussion with the following:

1. How did you learn from your role?

2. Did anyone's value change?

PART 2 – DIRECTIONS FOR FACILITATOR:

FACILITATOR NOTE: Now that they have identified what is really important, they will now explore how they actually experience their values. Part 2 is especially helpful for one on one coaching, and may not apply to a larger group. If Part 2 does not apply to your group, move to Part 3.

SCRIPT: Now that we have worked through one value, now think about when you experience the core value and what you get from it.

1. What do you feel?
2. Where do you experience it in your body (location of feeling)?
3. What do you hear?
4. What do you see?

DEBRIEF: It's important to know when you are really in sync with your values. Because when you are aware of these feelings, when you interacting with another and you are feeling that same resonance, then you have a possible Networlding partner.

PART 3 – DIRECTIONS FOR FACILITATOR:

SCRIPT: So far we have looked at one value, and then reflected on what actually happens internally when we experience that value. Now I would like to complete a list of **four value priorities.** You are welcome to use the list in your guide for examples, but don't feel obligated to use those words. The words aren't that important - it's important to make sure the words you choose for your values have meaning to you.

Once you have identified your top 4 values, look for the graphic of a house in your guide. Now, list your value priorities (in order if possible) in boxes 1-4. These values represent the foundation on which your structure is built. You will see as we move through the next sections how your values, strengths, goals, and actions create the structure for which you can apply the principles and steps of Networlding.

FACILITATOR NOTE: Below is the graphic participants will see in their guide.

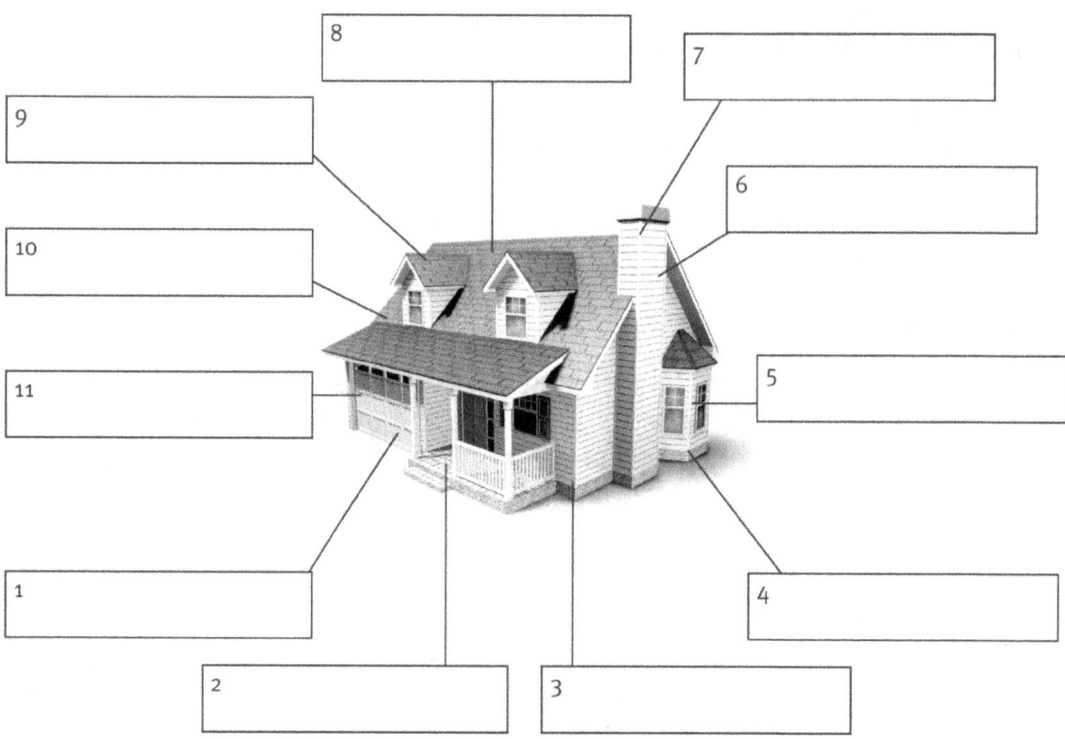

EXERCISE 2 – IDENTIFY YOUR STRENGTHS, GOALS, AND ACTIONS

FACILITATOR NOTE: Allow about 20 minutes total for this exercise. This exercise is divided into 2 parts. The first part is strengths, and the second part is goals and actions.

PART 1 – STRENGTHS

SCRIPT: Now let's take a look at **strengths**. Like your value priorities, strengths are a key component to your Networlding house. Strengths are those traits that best help us move forward in achieving our goals. They are qualities that come from you and contribute to your uniqueness. Uniqueness is what will set you apart; it helps you to be viewed as an influencer in your area of expertise.

DIRECTIONS FOR FACILITATOR AND SCRIPT:

1. Ask the participants to reflect on the following questions listed in their guide.
    a. What makes you unique?
    b. What do you love to do?
    c. What do you do better than anyone else?
    d. What resources (your own and from others) do you have available to you?
    e. What do people that you know you well see as your strengths?
    f. How would others that you trust describe you?

2. After reflecting on those questions, ask them to list their top 3 strengths. It might be helpful to consider strengths in the context of your environment where you spend a lot of time. For example, if you are researcher and spend time with others in the same role, what make you stand out? In other words, avoid confusing a current professional or personal role as a strength, but see where your uniqueness shines.

3. Fill those strengths into boxes 5-7.

22

PART 2 – GOALS AND ACTION STEPS

SCRIPT: So far we have taken a look at our value priorities and strengths - and we've done quite a bit of internal work to help us identify those pieces.

Now, let's take a look at **goals**. We can set Networlding goals now that we're aware of our most important values and strengths. Our goals represent the above-ground structure of the house.

We've all done goal-setting exercises before.

- What prevents us from achieving goals?

FACILITATOR NOTE: Allow time to answer.

Many times we set goals based on what's logical - what we think we should be doing or what we think others expect from us. Sometimes we aren't held accountable to the goal, so we don't achieve it.
When considering your goal, it might be a professional goal like meeting a quarterly objective, or a personal goal like becoming more involved in a volunteer organization.

As far as a timeframe goes, that is up to you. I would recommend looking at nothing longer than a yearly goal.

There are two stipulations for the goal:

1. It must be consistent with your values and be specific - something you can get fired up about!

2. It must be realistic to either achieve the goal or make significant progress on in the next 60-90 days. I'd like for you to set one goal and enter that into box 8.

FACILITATOR NOTE: Allow them several minutes to come up with a goal and enter it into their guide.

SCRIPT: We now have the foundation of our house, our values, and the above-ground structure of our house, our strengths and goals.
Now we can move on to **actions** - the steps we take to achieve the goals.

There are three boxes (#9-11) for you to play with actions. Let's take the opportunity to brainstorm with our tablemates. Spend the next 10 minutes sharing with one another (as you feel comfortable) your values, strengths and the goal you've set.

Help one another with some actionable ideas - sometimes it takes an outside perspective to help us with our strategies. You might also brainstorm any potential roadblocks and how to get around them.

Fill in some action step possibilities in boxes 9-11.

DEBRIEF:

1. Ask the participants if they're willing to share the "house" they've built.

2. Ask them to share any insights from the overall lesson.

3. Mention that what they have done in sharing with their tablemates has shared emotional support, informational support, and potentially some knowledge support, all steps within the Support Exchange model.

4. Ask for any closing comments or questions before moving to the next lesson.

LESSON 2 - NETWORLDING BELIEFS (20-30 MINUTES)

SCRIPT: When you begin networking with others in a values-based way (like the house you just built), you will naturally be led to others who are pursuing their goals based on values. Those people will also be naturally attracted to you.

Think of your Networld like a web. A web has many different points. These points represent your connections. Picture yourself in the center of the web. Those points are varying degrees of distance from the center and create circles, or your Networlding circles.

And what holds the Networld web together?

FACILITATOR NOTE: Allow time to answer. **Answer is beliefs.** This graphic is also in the participant guide.

SCRIPT: What are the Networlding beliefs? You will find some blank spaces in your participant workbook to fill these in.

FACILITATOR NOTE: There are blanks in the participant guide that correspond with these 6 beliefs. As an option, you may ask them to capture their ideas on a whiteboard or flipchart prior to providing these beliefs. <u>**Answers are underlined below in bold.**</u>

1. **<u>Anything is possible with the support of others.</u>** Networlders don't go it alone, and especially in this 2.0 world. Values-based goals are rarely, if ever, achieved by one person alone. Relationships are what help achieve greatness.

2. **<u>It's important to make a difference.</u>** Making a difference means affecting others in a significant, meaningful way. It's not surprising that Networlders serve in a volunteer capacity for causes they are passionate about. And a side benefit to that is a diverse Networld, plus the chance to demonstrate skills and knowledge to a new group of people.

3. **<u>You get what you ask for.</u>** Networlders are willing to ask for what they need to achieve a goal. Not only do Networlders ask, but they are also willing to give a significant amount in return.

4. **<u>All resources will be provided to reach your goals.</u>** Have you ever had a goal, and the first thing you think is "How am I going to find what I need to make this happen? Where do I even start?" Networlders have an inherent belief that when they set a goal, and deeply believe in that goal, that the right resources are out there to achieve it. This doesn't mean they believe resources will magically appear; what it means is that they are willing to put forth the effort and make the necessary relationships upfront that will lead them to the resources they need.

5. **<u>Life is filled with abundance and opportunities.</u>** Some traditional networkers operate on the assumption that there are certain places and situations reserved for making connections and doing business. In contrast, Networlders operate from an abundance mindset - and that opens them up to all sorts of opportunities. They recognize that relationships are formed in many places - as a result they often form more abundant connections.

6. **<u>There must be mutual rewards for partners.</u>** In a Networld, mutual rewards always outweigh individual rewards. Networlders are always thinking about how they can help the others in their Networld. Networlding partners are highly respectful of one another and believe that when everyone wins the partnership is strengthened.

CLOSING DISCUSSION: Ask the class to share any examples of where they have seen these beliefs in action.

- Examples could include business, volunteer, or community initiatives where they have seen or benefited from these values. They might also share an example of where these beliefs weren't in place and the outcomes.

- Be prepared to have an example of your own to share.

- You may summarize the main points of this step before moving to step 2.

STEP 2 – MAKE CONNECTIONS FOR YOUR PRIMARY CIRCLE

The second step in Networlding is making connections for your primary circle. This step builds upon the values identified in step 1. In step 2, participants will begin to create a list of potential Networld connections and then winnow it down to its essence based on emotional, business, cognitive, and value factors.

For this segment, you may want a flip chart or whiteboard. Participants have a corresponding guide to follow along. Take time to familiarize yourself with the participant guide.

AGENDA

Customize the agenda timing as needed.

TIME	ACTION	OBJECTIVE
5 minutes	Introduce Step 2	Communicate objectives
10 minutes	Review of Introduction and Step 1	Reinforce concepts from previous steps
10-15 minutes	**Lesson 1**: Contacts vs. Connections	Reinforce networking vs. Networlding; shift perspective from contacts to connections
30-40 minutes	**Lesson 2**: Creating Your Primary Circle	Create list for primary circle

OBJECTIVES

The objectives for step 2:

- A review of what was covered in the introduction and step 1
- Differentiate between a contact and connection
- Identify the qualities we want in a Networlding partner
- Create your primary circle

INTRODUCTION AND REVIEW (15 MINUTES)

SCRIPT: The second step in Networlding is making connections for your primary circle. This step builds upon the values identified in step 1. In step 2, participants will begin to create a list of potential Networld connections and then winnow it down to its essence based on emotional, business, cognitive, and value factors.

In this lesson, we will:

- Review of what was covered in the introduction and step 1
- Differentiate between a contact and connection
- Identify the qualities we want in a Networlding partner
- Create your primary circle

FACILITATOR NOTE: If you are moving directly from step 1 to step 2 (for example, in a day-long setting or bootcamp), you may opt to skip this review. If there is a time lapse between steps 1 and 2 (for example, in a weekly setting), this review will help re-focus the participants.

REVIEW

DIRECTIONS FOR FACILITATOR: Use this time to create a group conversation by asking any of the questions below.

Below is a sampling of questions; customize this review to fit your needs. Questions address material covered in the introduction or step 1.

- What are 3 traits of a networker?
- What are 3 traits of a Networlder?
- What are the 4 phases of the Networlding continuum?
- What should our goals be when improving our Networlding IQ?
- What are 3 key actions we can take to improve our Networld IQ?
- What is step 1 in creating your Networld?
- In step 1, what are the key steps to building your house?
- What two things do you need to identify to find your passion?
- What are your Networlding values?
- What are the two stipulations for setting a goal?
- What holds your Networld web together?
- What are 3 Networlding beliefs?

LESSON 1 – CONTACTS VS. CONNECTIONS (10-15 MINUTES)

SCRIPT: Identifying our values is the first step to establishing the deeper connections that Networlding requires. But relationships won't magically appear because we've identified what we value - from there, we have to identify compatible people with whom we can proactively create values-based relationships.

Let's begin by talking about the difference between a contact and connection.

FACILITATOR NOTE: Ask the class for their perspective on the differences, and then describe how these parallel networking vs. Networlding. (Some examples have been filled in below). Also ask the class to describe a personal experience or story of a contact versus connection. You should be prepared to share a story as well if needed.

Contact	Connection
May be temporary for a specific opportunity	Lasts beyond one opportunity
May not share the same values	Most likely shares the same values
Is probably part of an outlying circle	Probably part of your primary circle
Lower degree of trust	Higher degree of trust
Someone you might run into periodically	Someone you make a concerted effort to remain in contact with

DEBRIEF: There are few key points to remember when looking at contacts versus connections.

- Networlders spend more time building a relatively small number of strong relationships that will ultimately produce better opportunities and meaningful results.

- Discernment is key. Networlders form thoughtful relationships based on what will be exchanged. Will support be exchanged? Can you see that other person valuing the support exchange model? Is this person open to different relationship possibilities?

LESSON 2 – CREATING YOUR PRIMARY CIRCLE (30-40 MINUTES)

SCRIPT: There are 4 basic steps to creating a values-based primary circle. You can follow along in your participant guide.

1. Identify your current contacts.
2. Identify the qualities you want in a Networlding partner.
3. Analyze and assess.
4. Refine your top 5.

1. Identify your current contacts.

SCRIPT: The first step is to **identify your current contacts.** Our first instinct is sometimes to think only of business contacts, but open your mind to the possibilities of both professional and personal contacts. This holistic view gives you an exponentially greater pool of potential Networlders.

Using the baseline categories in your participant guide, take a few minutes to start listing out some contacts. We won't take time for an exhaustive list, but it should get you off to a good start so you can continue on your own.

You probably have a decently-sized list right now, even with the short amount of time we've spent on it. So how do we narrow that down?

2. Identify the qualities you want in a Networlding partner.

SCRIPT: We do that in the second step, which is to**identify the qualities you want in a Networlder.**Begin by looking back at the house you created in step 1.

- Look again at your values, and the goal you've set for yourself. You might begin your list in the context of that goal.

- Now think about people with whom you've had successful ventures, both professional and personal. This could be someone you partnered with on a client project, or your workout buddy that helped you train for the race you completed. Open your mind to the possibilities here.

So now, back in your guide follow these steps.

1. Take the next few minutes to begin a list of no more than **10 people** with whom you've achieved that kind of success together or someone who supported you in accomplishing something.

2. Next to each person's name, **list the qualities you value most about that person.** Think about what made you add that person to your list.

3. Reflect on all of those qualities you've listed. **Select one** that stands out to you as the one you most admire.

4. Now **select two additional qualities** from that list. (There will now be a total of 3 qualities.)

5. Which of these qualities mesh with your own? For example, if the top quality you admire is visionary thinking, and you are strong with logistics, those two qualities may mesh to make the vision happen.

DEBRIEF: Ask for some volunteers in the class to describe their lists:

- Type of people on the list (friends, family, professional)
- Top quality they value in their list
- How their top choices mesh with their own qualities

SCRIPT: So how do you recognize a good Networlder when you meet one? In your guide, there is space for you to fill in these blanks.

FACILITATOR NOTE: Before filling in the blanks for them, you might ask the class what they think makes a good Networlder and see what they already know. You might also ask them to describe these traits first before providing the detailed explanations below. **Answers for blanks are in bold below.**

A good Networlder is:

1. **Supportive.** Networlders support your success; they listen and encourage.

2. **A continuous communicator.** A Networlder keeps in regular contact with his/her circle, whether or not there's an opportunity out there.

3. **Reliable and responsible.** Networlders deliver on their promises and take their responsibilities seriously.

4. **Influential.** Influence isn't necessarily based on wealth or prestige. In a Networld it's usually experience and expertise. Networlders are usually well-respected and are willing to use their influence on behalf of their partners.

5. **Knowledgeable.** Networlders have rich and varied experiences. Knowledge exchange between Networlders goes beyond information exchange - they share their real-world experiences, lessons learned, and wisdom.

6. **An active listener.** In today's multi-tasking world, many people aren't truly listening because there is so much competing for our attention and energy. But Networlders are attentive, and they try to understand where

7. the other person is coming from and offer feedback that reflects this understanding.

8. **Empathic.** Empathy goes hand-in-hand with active listening. It's the ability to put yourself in another person's shoes and try to reallyunderstand what that person might be going through. Networlders know that the person comes before the opportunity, and never to take advantage of another.

9. **Appreciative.** This one is often overlooked, because in today's world people don't show enough appreciation for others. A Networlder truly appreciates the others around him or her and regularly expresses gratitude. It might be a hand-written thank you note or an email. Small acts of appreciation build up a wealth of good will that goes a long way. Do you know someone that you would do anything for? Probably because they show appreciation for what you do for them.

10. **Connection-conscious.** Do you know someone who has a knack for seeing and making connections? They recognize when two people should be introduced and act on it. This Networlder might connect two people with similar personal interests, or bring people together to achieve a specific goal.

3. Analyze and assess.

SCRIPT: So far we have talked about identifying your contacts and the qualities you value in your list of ten. We've also talked about the top qualities of Networlders.

Next, you'll want to **analyze and assess**to determine three key things about your primary circle. Is the person:

1. An exchanger? Exchangers:

   - Demonstrate a concern for your issues and needs
   - Attempt to make sure there's an equal exchange of information and leads
   - Make an effort to stay in touch with you.
   - Provide assistance without ever talking about how much they're doing for you or keeping score.

2. Someone with whom you can establish an emotional connection?

3. Someone you will enjoy working with?

4. Refine to your top 5.

SCRIPT: Lastly, you'll want to **refine your list to the top 5, your primary circle.** We're going to spend the next 10 minutes refining our lists. Even if you don't finish here, you should have a good start to finish on your own.

In your guide you'll see a space for your connections. Next to each connection jot down the status of your relationship, and the next action step you will take with that person.

You will also see a few helpful suggestions to keep in mind when creating your list.

FACILITATOR NOTE: Suggestions are from page 69 in the hardcover book and are listed in the participant guide. The graphic on the following page is in the participant guide; point that out to the class.

DEBRIEF: Ask for volunteers to share insights about their primary circle, with questions such as:

1. How many connections are in your primary circle?
2. What challenges did you have in creating your circle?
3. Do you notice any patterns about the connections in your circle?
4. How many influencers and bridgers are in your circle?
5. What actions can you see yourself taking right away to make this circle as effective as possible?

CLOSING DISCUSSION: You may ask for further questions, comments, or takeaways from the class. You may also summarize the key points before moving to step 3.

STEP 3 – EXPAND YOUR CIRCLES

The third step in Networlding is expanding your connections for your primary circle. While the primary circle is a Networlder's main center of influence, he or she will also need secondary and tertiary circles to architect their Networld.

For this segment, you may want a flip chart or whiteboard. Participants have a corresponding guide to follow along. Take time to familiarize yourself with the participant guide.

AGENDA

Customize the agenda timing as needed.

TIME	ACTION	OBJECTIVE
5 minutes	Introduce Step 3	Communicate objectives
15 minutes	Icebreaker/Review	Review to reinforce concepts from previous week; forge new connections in group setting
30 minutes	**Lesson 1**: The Value of Influencers	Understand qualities of influencers and how to reach them
15 minutes	**Lesson 2**: Secondary and Tertiary Circles	Expand beyond primary circles
10 minutes	**Exercise 1:** Creating Secondary and Tertiary circles	Expand beyond primary circles

OBJECTIVES

The objectives for step 3:

- A review of what has been covered so far in previous steps
- We'll learn about influencers: who they are, why they are important to your Networld, and how to reach them
- Creating secondary and tertiary circles

INTRODUCTION AND REVIEW (15-20 MINUTES)

SCRIPT: Welcome to Networlding Step 3: Expanding your circles. In step 2 you created your primary circle. Think of your primary circle as your first circle of influence. But you will also have secondary and tertiary circles of influence – that while less important than your primary one, they are still significant.

In this lesson, we will:

- Review of what has been covered so far in previous steps
- Uncover influencers: who they are, why they are important to your Networld, and how to reach them
- Create secondary and tertiary circles

This opening activity will provide a review of the concepts we've learned and applied so far.

REVIEW

FACILITATOR NOTE: This activity is best suited for the group if they have had time away (for example, in a weekly workshop format) to absorb and apply the lessons in their life. However, it can still apply even if you are moving between steps more quickly as part of a 1- or 2-day workshop (the answers just may not be as in-depth).

DIRECTIONS FOR FACILITATOR: At group tables, ask people to pair up. There may be groups of 3 for odd numbers. As an extra step, you may even ask people to select a new table to sit at so they are able to expand their connections (Networlding in action!).

SCRIPT: As a pair or group you will ask these questions of one another. They are also in your participant guide. Use active listening and take notes, because you will be asked to share the information your partner gave you.

1. What is your top Networlding value and why? (From Step 1)
2. Which Networlding qualities do you most value in your connections and why? (From Step 2)

3. How has your work here so far helped you move toward the goal you set out to do? (Intro - house analogy)

DEBRIEF: Ask several pairs to share their partner's story. This demonstrates active listening, plus both emotional and information exchange. You most likely won't have time for everyone. Also ask others (ideally those who didn't volunteer) to share any other stories or insights they have learned from the Networlding process so far.

LESSON 1 – THE VALUE OF INFLUENCERS (30 MINUTES)

SCRIPT: So far we have talked about the first two steps in Networlding: establishing your values and creating your primary circle. In this step we'll have the opportunity to expand our circles.

Why do we do this? Because chances are good that out of the list you created in step 2, many people aren't good Networlding candidates for one reason or another. You may need to go outside of your connections to complete your primary circle.

But the list of potential Networlding partners is you do is gold, and will also have will also have connections to others you may not know.

We'll cover three points in this lesson:

1. The **importance of influencers** in our Networld.

2. The **common behaviors influential Networlders exhibit**.

3. How **we identify and reach influencers.**

Let's start by talking about the **importance of influencers (1).**

DISCUSSION: Ask the class these questions and open it up for discussion.

FACILITATOR NOTE: You may want to use a flipchart to capture answers. You may also want to have a personal story of an influencer in your life that you're ready to share.

- What does influence mean to you?

- What does power mean to you? How are influence and power different?

- How do you think influence differs between a networking perspective and a Networlding perspective?

- Where have you found influencers in unusual places or situations?

DEBRIEF/SCRIPT: There are few key points to remember when understanding the importance of influence as it relates to Networlding. You can take notes in your guide.

1. Networlding defines influence as the power to affect another person, people, or course of events.

2. Networlders may have position or wealth, but they also have *earned influence* - their power to influence comes from a particular set of skills, knowledge, or experience. They aren't necessary title holders.

3. Networlding influencers are doers, not passive observers. They always add value.

4. Influencers actively work on their Networlding partners' behalf, making valuable connections, sharing resources, and making recommendations.

SCRIPT: We'll move on next to the **common behaviors that influential Networlders typically have (2).** There is space for you to enter these in your guide.

FACILITATOR NOTE: These are fill-in-the-blank in the student guide, so be sure to articulate all six.

1. **Willingness to give.** They are known for being generous with their time and resources and their influence is a direct result of how much they contribute to individuals and teams. Their impact stems from their willingness to share ideas, knowledge, and information that can create opportunities.

2. **Community involvement.** This is one of the most important traits for a Networlder and an influencer. Influencers purposefully expand their horizons beyond professional connections. You'll find them in volunteer organizations, heading up committees, etc. Influencers realize they can make a difference.

3. **Awareness of others' needs and interests.** Influencers routinely think beyond their own needs. That influence stems from being proactive in anticipating and responding to others - ultimately that builds trust.

4. **Dependability.** We all know dependable (and not so dependable) people. Influencers? They're dependable - they do what they say they'll do, there are no surprises.

5. **Persistence.** People who make the most impact are those that don't give up. Persistence earns respect and influence because people know that person will stick with an issue or opportunity in good times and bad.

6. **Covisioning.** Covisioning is a willingness to blend one's vision with someone else's rather than insisting on a singular vision of how things should be. In many respects, a solo visionary is a symbol of networking past.

SCRIPT: So far we have talked about our perceptions of influence and some keys to remember when understanding Networlding influencers. We've also talked about six behaviors that Networlding influencers exhibit. Are they any other questions or comments before we move on?

Now we're going to talk about how **we identify influencers and then reach them (3).** Influencers aren't always easy to identify - there are many giving, community-minded, dependable people in the world. But the truth is many of them don't make an impact.

It's important to remember that impact and influence go hand in hand. Impact comes from a few attributes, and influencers have at least one of five attributes in spades.

FACILITATOR NOTE: You may want to ask participants for what they think these five attributes are before providing them. This will help you (and them) to gauge what they already know as well as provide new information. As you go, you may want to ask for stories from participants that demonstrate these attributes, or have a story or two of your own to share. These are NOT fill-in-the-blank.

1. **Broad base of knowledge.** The broader the base of knowledge, the more influential someone can be. A broad base of knowledge means that the person has knowledge of an unusually wide range of information. Most people are experts in a very narrow field. But some have knowledge that crosses boundaries. The most key element here is that these influencers with a broad base of knowledge **do** something with that knowledge - they don't just sit on it.

    - <u>Here's how you can take action</u>: When you meet others, look for conversational signs that they could have a broad knowledge base. Be careful to discern whether they are just good conversationalists or if they really are knowledgeable - a few probing questions will work. If their answers are shallow or evasive, that's a sign they lack the body of knowledge that influencers have.
    - Can you think of anyone in your life that has this attribute?

2. **Large perspective.** Influencers are big thinkers. They see possibilities where others don't. A large perspective can take many shapes. It might be a person we think of as a big visionary, but it may also be the person who takes a very complex subject and make it understandable and meaningful for others. A big thinker may not be always on the money, but they generate fresh ideas, and they aren't afraid to express them.

    - <u>Here's how you can take action</u>: Be conscious of people who surprise you with their insights. Note how they view the world and its possibilities in a different light.

- Who do you know that's a big thinker with a large perspective?

3. **Difference makers.** Typically we associate difference-makers with high office. But look for people who use their difference-making platforms to *help others.* They help others grow their careers, they create mutually beneficial opportunities, alliances, and collaborative partnerships. Your primary circle shouldn't have only difference makers, but it's helpful to at least one person with this attribute.

   - **Mini-activity: (FACILITATOR NOTE**: Allow about 5 minutes for this mini-activity. You might ask the class to share some of their names, and if they are stuck on how to reach them ask other participants to share ideas. You might also share a personal story of how you reached out to a difference maker.)

     1. I'd like you to take a few minutes to create a list of people you might contact who are highly visible in your community or industry. This is a brainstorming list, so jot down everyone that comes to mind without judgment.
     2. Next, place a star next to those that you think have the traits of Networlders and the behaviors of influencers.
     3. From that short list, select 2-3 that you would like to contact and list one way to accomplish that.

4. **Active in organizations.** Influencers are frequently involved in a variety of trade associations, community groups, volunteer organizations, and so on. *Involvement* is the operative word here. Many people join organizations and then never actively contribute. Influencers do, and their level of activity carries weight with people and is usually shown in the variety of relationships they establish.
   - Can you think of an influencer who is actively involved in an organization, and what have you learned from that person?

   - <u>Here's how you can take action:</u> Think of a group you would like to join that truly interests you and does things you believe are worthwhile. It can be either professional or personal. Next, determine if there is a group member that has Networlding qualities or influencer qualities. If there is it makes sense to join the group and make that person's acquaintance. However, make sure you're not joining the group solely to meet someone.

5. **Skilled communicators.** Some people derive their influence from their ability to communicate with others, be it public speaking, writing, internet marketing, public relations, etc. Communications is a broad term, but we know that skilled communicators can definitely effect motivated action in others.

- Is there a skilled communicator (can be well-known or otherwise) that has personally influenced you?

- Here's how you can take action: Determine what communication skills you lack in reaching the goal you set to achieve (back to the house). Create a list of people who possess those skills - you may need to do a bit of research here based on what you need. For example, do you want to launch a community blog but don't know where to start? You might research other blogs, looking for patterns and reputable people as potential contacts.

SCRIPT: We've discovered the five attributes of influencers, and we know that influencers have at least one - if not several. So how do find them and **then reach them**?**(3)**

FACILITATOR NOTE: You may want to ask participants for their input on where to find influencers. This will help you (and them) to gauge what they already know as well as provide new information. As you go, you may want to ask for stories from participants where they found an influential person, or have a story or two of your own to share.

1. **Internet.** Use keyword searches for your industry to find thought leaders. When you get to know an influencer through his or her work, you might email that person or seek them out through social media. You can send them a note supporting their ideas and begin establishing a loose relationship. Social media especially has opened the doors to connecting with people that would be otherwise difficult to reach.

2. **Periodicals.** Networlders are well-read, so you'll want to search for both online and offline publications, newspapers, books, and article directories. These are great ways to find potential influencers, and many of them may have contact information within those publications.

3. **Conferences and lectures.** When you attend a conference, keynote, or lecture do you introduce yourself to that person whenever possible? If not, you're missing a great opportunity.

   - One idea is to write a question related to the talk on the back of your business card and approach the speaker after the event. Talk with the speaker, telling him or her you enjoyed the speech and that you wrote down a question you'd like to discuss for a few minutes at some point in the next several weeks. Follow up and keep any discussion to the short time your promised. This shows your respect of that person's time, and can set the stage for future exchanges.

4. **Volunteering.** Volunteering pays off in connections when it's done from the heart. When you volunteer for a group or organization that you strongly believe in, a few things will happen. One, you're likely to support that group or organization for the long-term - allowing you to create better connections. Two, when you do meet an influencer and establish a connection at a volunteer level doing something you both love, that connection will strong and meaningful to the influencer. Some of the best opportunities in business and life come from connections based on personal interests.

5. **Program committees.** When you join an industry association, make every effort to get actively involved. The group's programming committee is a very visible place to start because you'll be connecting with influencers in that industry on a regular basis. You will also be creating continual value for the
group with quality programming, and have further qualified access to group members.

6. **Lists, Directories, Alumni Groups**. Your alumni directory is a great place to start because you will already have a least somewhat warm connection if you choose to research and reach out to any people you think are influencers.

   - Use your LinkedIn groups as well. If you locate someone you think might be an influencer, look to see what other groups that person is involved in - when you share a group designation in LinkedIn, you can reach out directly to that person even if you aren't a first-degree connection.

7. **Traveling.** Use airline travel to its fullest! A lot of great conversations can be struck up at 35,000 feet. Just be careful to respect their desire to be left alone.

8. **Leisure activities.** People are sometimes mistaken that you can only meet influencers in work-related situations. Be open to meeting people in your personal activities as well. As with volunteering, some of the best connections are made when personal interests are shared. Now these people may not be influencers, but they can become a great friend, which adds balance to your Networld. And you never know when that same person can connect you with someone else of great influence!

9. **Current connections.** Everyone has hidden connections, that don't become apparent until we do some exploration. There's a psychological principle known as the "horizon of observability." In Networlding it means that sometimes we have difficulty seeing beyond our current connections. If you think of relationships as links in a chain, we don't see beyond those directly linked to us - when in reality we are connected to many other links - we just don't see it because it's not a direct connection.

- Social media sites like LinkedIn can help "break the chain" because when you have first degree connection to someone, you also get indirect access to second and third degree connections - your "horizon of possibility."

- Sometimes what it takes is an in-depth conversation with a current connection to be granted access to their hidden connections. You must first be willing to share a significant piece of information about yourself. All of the people you know and have formed a bond with have at least one influencer among their hidden connections.

LESSON 2 – SECONDARY AND TERTIARY CIRCLES (15 MINUTES)

SCRIPT: We've spent a significant amount of time here discussing influencers because they can play such an important role in our Networld. We're going to combine what we've learned in this step, along with step 2 where we created our primary circle.

After we finish here, you will hopefully have a broader vision of your Networlding possibilities by expanding your circles. We'll first discuss secondary and tertiary circles, and then you will get some time to work in your guide actually creating them (or at the least the beginnings of them).

FACILITATOR NOTE: The points to follow are all listed in the participant guide so participants can follow along and take notes.

SCRIPT: Back in step 2, we started the process of creating our primary circle. In your **primary circle**:

1. You have no more than 5 people.

2. You have partners whose values are compatible with yours.

3. Circle members manifest the behaviors and attributes of a Networlder.

4. Your partners have some ability to influence. Otherwise they are candidates better suited for your secondary circle.

5. Your main task is to develop and deepen relationships with this group.

6. Your partners are people who you interact with on a regular basis and feel closeness to - more so than those in your secondary circles.

Now expanding to your **secondary circle**, these people:

1. Have fewer values in common with you than people in your primary group.

2. Possess goals that aren't completely aligned with your goals.

3. Have areas of interests that don't match up perfectly with your own.

4. Don't possess as many traits and behaviors of Networlders as those in your primary group.

5. Lack the time or interest to meet regularly or work together on many opportunities.

- Point #5 is very important, because it will help you with people "sitting on the fence" between your primary and secondary circles.

- Even if you have commonalities with someone that will make them a great primary circle member, if they lack the time or interest - you're ultimately wasting your time.

Additional points to remember with your secondary circle:

1. Add names to this group that you may have originally considered for your primary circle, but then omitted.

2. This group doesn't have to be limited to 10, so there's more margin for error.

3. Your secondary circle is a prime place to fill in any gaps in your primary circle. Add diversity that you may be missing in your primary circle to this group. This could mean skills, age, sex, ethnicity, etc.

4. It's possible that those who you initially thought would be ideal Networlders for your primary circle may no longer be a good fit for any number of reasons. An incident might make your doubt their values, or they may become involved in other interests. These individuals may be better suited to your secondary circle.

Moving to your **tertiary circle,** this group:

1. Is wide, shallow, and full of weak contacts.

2. Is often composed of exchanges involving basic information such as job openings, data, statistics, etc.

3. Usually consists of people who don't want anything beyond an information relationship (at least at this time). They may be extremely busy and don't have time devote to a relationship with you, or they may lack the experience and maturity necessary for a mutually beneficial partnership.

4. In a sense, are classic networkers. They may develop someday into Networlding relationships, but for now they are best suited to a tertiary relationship.

EXERCISE 1 – CREATING YOUR SECONDARY AND TERTIARY CIRCLES (10-15 MINUTES)

SCRIPT: In this exercise, you will have an opportunity to begin creating your secondary and tertiary circles. In your participant guide you will see:

- A flow chart to help you form your circles
- A visual to help to form your three circles (transfer your primary circle connections from step 2)

FACILITATOR NOTE: Allow the group about 10 minutes to work on this. It won't be enough time to complete the activity, but will give them a start in completing it on their own. If you have allotted sufficient time for the group to complete, tailor this timing to your situation.

The full activity as shown in the participant's guide is on the following page for you to follow along. Close this activity with the debrief questions.

DEBRIEF: Ask the class to share their experience in creating their secondary and tertiary circles. You may use the following questions to guide the discussion:

- What did you notice about your existing network?
- Where are you currently spending most of your relationship-building time?
- How might your results change if you follow the 80/20 rule of Networlding (shown in the circle graphic)?
- What role do you think social media and other relationship-building tools will play in your circles?

CLOSING DISCUSSION: Ask for any additional questions, comments, or takeaways that the class has uncovered before moving on to step 4. You may also summarize the main points.

Use the Networlding Circles Flowchart to help you decide your primary, secondary, and tertiary circles. Notice that it all begins with value priorities from step 1.

FORMING NETWORLDING CIRCLES FLOWCHART

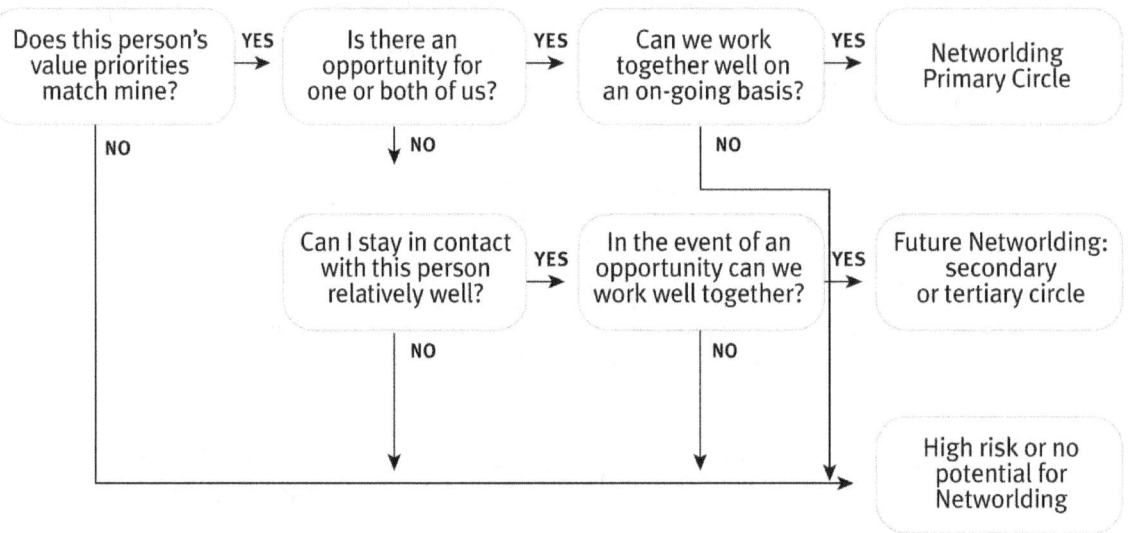

1. Your main task is to develop and deepen relationships with people you've assigned to your primary circle. Take the following steps:

   - Initiate contact with at least 3 people you consider prime candidates for your primary circle and who've determined to be influencers.

   - If the response is positive, schedule a meeting or lunch.

   - If the meeting goes well, schedule additional meetings to exchange ideas, information, feelings, and opportunities.

   - Tap into their hidden connections.

   - Continuously assess these 3 relationships to determine if they meet the criteria established for both Networlders and influencers.

Repeat these steps whenever possible to add to your primary circle and to replace any individual who no longer belongs to that circle.

2. Your next task is to create a list of people you've designated for your secondary and tertiary circles.

   - Stay aware of what the people in those circles are doing.

   - Occasionally communicate with them with an eye toward determining if they're ready and willing to move into your primary circle.

   - With your tertiary circle, keep the relationship on an informational basis.

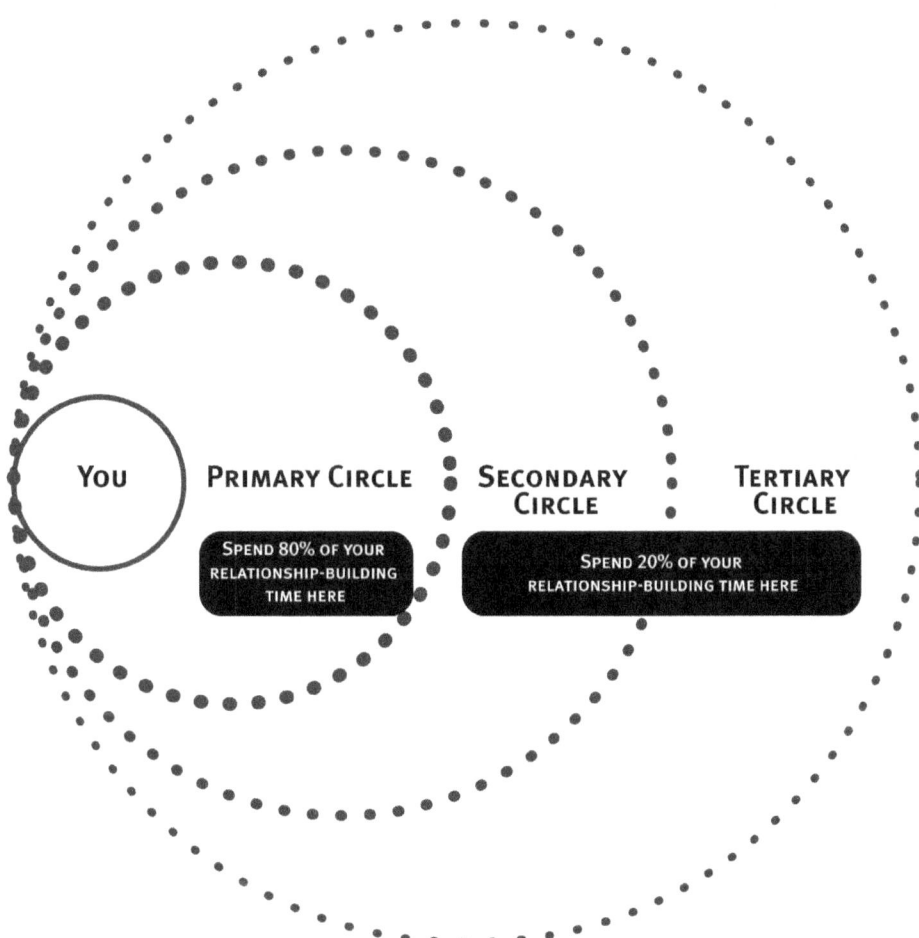

Enter names for your primary, secondary, and tertiary circles. You may already have some connections for your primary circle from step 2. Take time to refine those primary connections based on what you've learned about influencers.

Expect this list to be dynamic, changing over time. This exercise won't result in an exhaustive list, but will help shift your perspective to thinking in terms of Networlding circles and where you invest your relationship-building time.

Primary Circle	Secondary Circle	Tertiary Circle

STEP 4 – INITIATE EXCHANGING RELATIONSHIPS

The fourth step in Networlding is about initiating exchanging relationships. The objective of every aspiring Networlder should be to establish relationships with mutual exchange as the foundation.

For this segment, you may want a flip chart or whiteboard. Participants have a corresponding guide to follow along. Take time to familiarize yourself with the participant guide.

AGENDA

Customize the agenda timing as needed.

TIME	ACTION	OBJECTIVE
5 minutes	Introduction	Communicate overall objectives
10 minutes	**Review:**The Domino Effect	Reinforce previous concepts; forge new connections in group setting
15-20 minutes	**Lesson 1**: Support Exchange Model	Gain more familiarity with the support exchange model
15-20 minutes	**Lesson 2**: Ingredients of an Effective Exchange	Create effective exchanges and meaningful relationships
5 minutes	**Supplement:** Questions and Expressions of Support	Supplemental questions to help with structured support conversations

OBJECTIVES

The objectives for step 4:

- Reinforce the concepts covered so far in previous steps
- Explore the Support Exchange Model.
- Identify the ingredients of an effective exchange
- Uncover strategies for establishing meaningful contact

REVIEW – THE DOMINO EFFECT (10 MINUTES)

SCRIPT: This opening activity will provide a review of the Networlding terminology and concepts we've learned and applied so far. This will help further reinforce the importance of Networlding over networking and continue to shift your perspective toward value-based relationships.

FACILITATOR NOTE: This activity consists of a stack of 20-30 domino-type cards. Each card has a Networlding term on one end, and then the Networlding definition of another term on the other end. The activity is played using the rules of Dominoes, except that a player must lay a term against the correct definition or vice versa.

This activity can be run in small tables, or as a larger group. If it's run in small tables, you will need multiple sets of the domino cards. You may want to ask people to move tables for some new Networlding connections. If it's run in a large group, consider larger cards/print (for easier reading) and a central table where participants take turns matching the dominos. Samples are below:

Networlding	Horizon of Observability
The foreseeable number of people connected to those whom are connected to millions through our relationships with even just a few people.	

DIRECTIONS FOR FACILITATOR: Determine if you will run this activity at tables or as a large group. Time the activity, allowing 5-7 minutes for the table or group
to complete.

DEBRIEF: Ask the group(s) how they did with the terminology. Time permitting, you may review all terminology, or any terms where there are specific questions. Point out that using the terminology will continue to shift their perspective toward value-based relationships.

LESSON 1 – SUPPORT EXCHANGE MODEL (15 MINUTES)

SCRIPT: So far we have covered three steps in the Networlding process: establishing your values, creating your primary circle, and expanding our circles.

So how do we keep all of our circles active and balanced? It's by creating relationships of exchange. More specifically as a Networlder, you need to take the initiative in establishing and creating an environment for the exchange.

There are two big challenges any Networlder faces in initiating relationships:

1. Exchanging various forms of support
2. Developing trust

FACILITATOR NOTE: You may want to use a flipchart to draw the exchange model pyramid while explaining the emotional, informational, knowledge, and promotional exchanges.

SCRIPT: The support exchange model mirrors the hierarchical process involved in building any meaningful relationship. Just by looking at the entire pyramid, you can probably think of some relationships in your own business and life that have naturally modeled that flow.

There are 7 levels in the support exchange model. Within this step however we're going to cover four and the others will be covered more in detail in Networlding steps to follow. Follow along in your guide.

FACILITATOR NOTE: There are fill-in-the-blanks in the student guide (and space for notes) for each of the 4 steps. You may also choose to review all 4 steps first before asking for examples.

1. **Emotional support.** This is the foundation of building a Networlding relationship. You may also think of it as emotional intelligence, which is the ability to understand emotions and use them to promote emotional and intellectual growth in yourself and others.

   People are increasingly receptive to emotional honesty, and they're looking for someone who not only says what he or she really feels, but is also an empathic listener. Emotional support builds trust and naturally allows the relationship to progress along the support exchange model.

2. **Informational support.** Once at least some kind of emotional exchange has been established, people are more willing to volunteer information. But let's face it - people are overwhelmed with data and information.

3. Think of all the sources you yourself have to gather information. The key here is obvious, easy-to-obtain information versus valuable not-as-well-known facts and statistics. Networlders who are especially good at information exchange are typically well-skilled in:

   - Discerning what's relevant when confronted with volumes of information.

   - Observing the world around them

   - Tuning into what type of information the other person needs.

4. **Knowledge support.** The next natural progression in relationship-building is knowledge support. There's a difference between knowledge and information. Information is typically pure data, while knowledge often means sharing ones conclusions, experiences, personal insights, and ideas. Knowledge support signifies a growing level of trust. Examples of knowledge sharing may be in mastermind groups or mentoring relationships.

5. **Promotional support.** This is one of the best ways to get a Networlding relationship off on the right foot. By consciously keeping an eye out for connections between people, you put yourself in the position of offering invaluable promotion support. Think about the people within your primary circle. Can you connect them with others, or refer their business skills to other Networlders? As you promote, so too you are promoted. It's a critical exchange you want to establish quickly within the relationships.

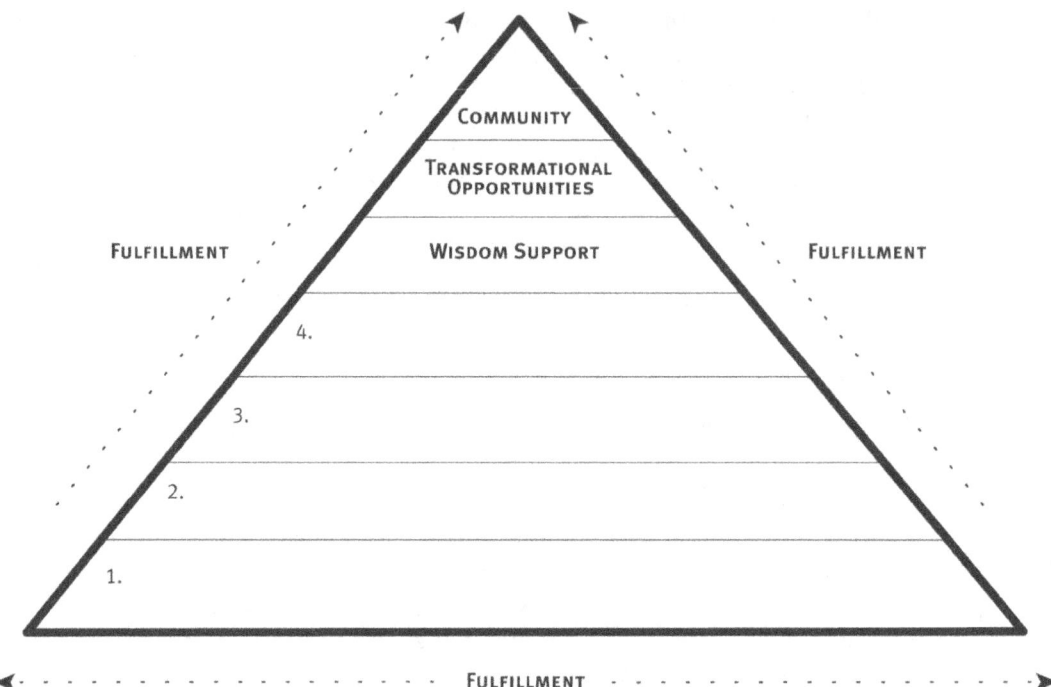

FACILITATOR NOTE: Once you've reviewed all 4 steps, ask the class for any personal stories or examples of where they have seen the steps progress. Be prepared to share your own story as well.

(FACILITATOR EXAMPLE: I met someone who is now a close member of my primary circle at a training-industry association meeting. We obviously had something in common because we were both in attendance and members of the association. After the meeting ended and people were socializing, we naturally introduced ourselves to one another and established that we were both business owners.

From there we exchanged business cards and agreed to meet to learn more about one another's business. After a positive first meeting and realizing we had a lot in common both personally and professionally, we began to share business ideas and connections with one another. We both introduce the other to valuable connections, and promote one another's business in the appropriate situations.)

LESSON 2 – INGREDIENTS OF AN EFFECTIVE EXCHANGE (15 MINUTES)

SCRIPT: We've spent some time talking about the first four steps in support exchange model. The remaining steps we will visit in more detail in upcoming steps.

You'll notice those steps covered the "*what*" of an exchange: emotion, information, knowledge, and promotion.

Now we'll talk about the "*how*" of an exchange.

Starting an effective exchange is all about trust. You need to trust one another sufficiently before there's a comfort level to share valuable ideas, information, and the other forms of support. Trust allows us to:

- Move past the rough spots of failed opportunities or disagreements

- Connect beyond a single business deal

- Create an environment of openness and honesty

Let's think about a cake recipe. It usually has a certain number of ingredients, and when correctly combined and baked, creates the wonderful finished desert.

And how well that cake turns out depends on many variables: the quality of the ingredients, the right amounts of each one, the right temperature, the right time, etc. When one of those variables is off, it doesn't turn out right.

The cake is your Networlding relationship. And there are certain trust ingredients that need to be combined to create a perfect cake, or a great relationship. And the transformational opportunities that will result - is of course the icing on the cake.

Let's go back to our ingredients of trust:

1. **Points of commonality.** The more common interests you share, the more potential there is for trust. Points of commonality establish a comfort level that is a pre-cursor to trust. They can include interests, skills, or hobbies. That's why often times a business relationship flows from shared personal interests. When initiating a relationship, find a way to communicate those interests that are most important to you.

2. **Points of credibility.** This isn't about bragging or name dropping. We all know people who do that and it's a real turn off. Instead this is about modestly and honestly communicating your contributions, strengths, and unique experiences. People tend to trust people who have achieved something unique or important - but are modest about it. Think about who you'd like to surround yourself with, those who you have credibility, or those who don't share their points of credibility?

OPTIONAL SHORT EXERCISE (3 MINUTES): Top Points of Commonality and Credibility

DIRECTIONS FOR FACILITATOR: At each table, ask participants to identify among themselves points of commonality and points of credibility. This will require them to ask open-ended questions of one another, and also honestly communicate their own accomplishments and strengths.

Allow about 3 minutes for this exercise. Then debrief by asking the table to share any points of commonality or credibility that led to further relationship building at the table and what they learned from the exercise.

3. **Matched values.** Shared values make a difference in building trust. Not everyone is comfortable explicitly expressing their values, but as you get to know someone you will be able to sense what's important to them. One way to explore this area to talk with other person about what's most meaningful in your life in work. When you explain what's important and why, they might be more willing to open up and share what's meaningful to them.

4. **Tone and timing.** Do you know someone who you'd consider an "anti-networlder?" Someone who's glib, slick, and superficial - says all the right things, but underneath it's not meaningful. That's why sincerity on your part in all relationships is critical, even when it's something that the other person may not want to hear. Timing is important as well. Be aware of your surroundings and of others - pay attention to when others might be open to a certain discussion, or when another time might be more appropriate.

5. **Matched communication styles.** Next time you're out and about, notice a group of people who seem very at ease with one another - you might notice they tend to use similar gestures, postures, and phrases. Likewise when speaking or meeting with someone, pay attention to their energy level, body language, vocal pitch, speed, and words. Try to match and mirror them as much as possible in a natural way, and notice that they may seem to be more open to you. This is a simple and effective technique to make another person feel as if you're speaking the same language.

6. **Etiquette.** These points may seem obvious, but any Networlder is careful to do the following:

- Follow-up every time and deliver on your promises.

- Maintain eye contact during conversations. It shows your sincerity and credibility.

- Smile! It shows you're open and eager to listen.

- Locate people who are standing alone and introduce yourself. It shows you're caring and compassionate.

- Give first before you ask for anything.

- Avoid social butterfly-itis. Spend a reasonable amount of time with people you initially meet.

- Be expressive. An interested, expressive face and body shows you're actively listening.

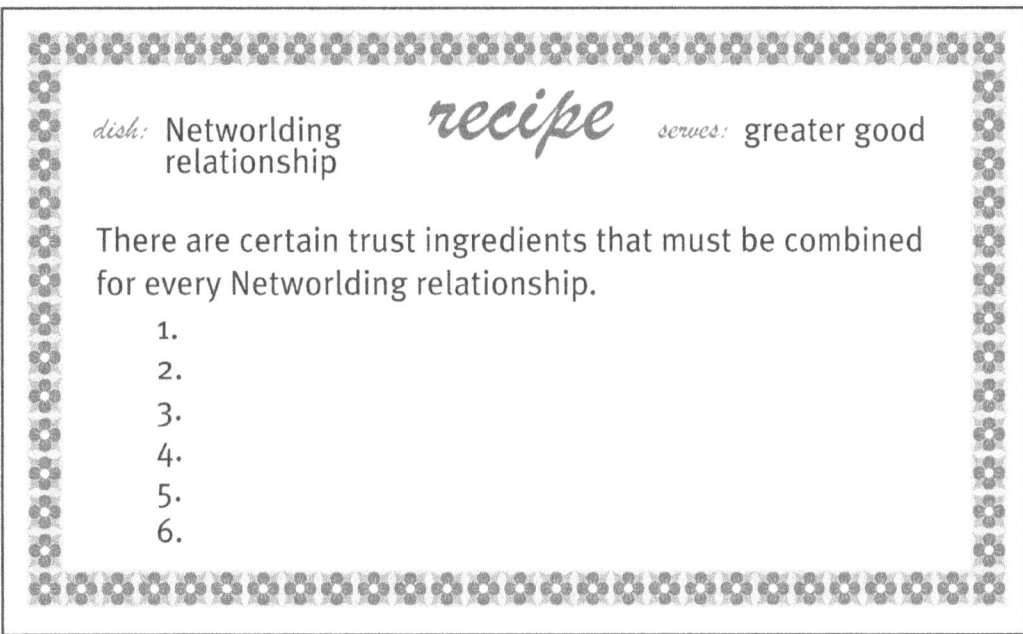

dish: Networlding relationship   *recipe*   *serves:* greater good

There are certain trust ingredients that must be combined for every Networlding relationship.

1.
2.
3.
4.
5.
6.

SCRIPT CONTINUES: So far we have talked about 4 of the 7 levels of exchanging support, and we've talked about trust as a key ingredient in creating those exchanges.

Now, we need to talk about specifically how you can begin to establish meaningful contact. No matter how outgoing or seasoned you may be in Networlding principles, it can be difficult to approach people.

Here are some specific tactics you can use to ease the path to initiating relationships. You can follow along in your participant guide.

FACILITATOR NOTE: You may ask participants to share any of their own tactics, or share an example of where one of these ideas worked for them. Be prepared to share an example of your own.

1. **Seek relationships in the "easiest" places first.** Look at all of the possible opportunities in front of you - events you are attending, volunteer activities, customer interactions - these are all opportunities for you to look for new relationships to build. Look at your "routine" activities in a new light.

2. **Always be prepared.** Never go into a relationship-building situation cold. Especially if it's an event where you will encounter a lot of unfamiliar faces. For example, if you are attending an event, make an effort to contact the event organizer to introduce yourself and ask a
couple of open-ended questions about the organization. This builds rapport, helps you learn more about the event/organization, and will give you more confidence.

3. **Seek connections even if you don't want to.** Accept the fact that there will be times when you just won't feel like reaching out to people. But ironically enough, these are often the times you make some of the best connections! Keep yourself in check by envisioning the incredible Networld you're constructing with these connections.

4. **Learn from rejection.** Rejection is a really common fear and holds people back from attempting to make a meaningful connection. It's not always easy to do, but try to look at rejection objectively and realize that some connections may just not happen as we want them to. It might help to write a short "anti-rejection" affirmation statement that helps you through those times. For example, "I'm a kind, honest person who sincerely wants to succeed and help others whenever possible."

5. **Create a positive image.** Remember, that you are your brand! Your appearance, attitude, and behaviors matter. It's your responsibility to project a positive image and attract others to you. Be aware of your words and actions around others. One simple way to project a positive image - smile sincerely!

6. **Build appreciation into your conversations with others.** Look for ways to sincerely show appreciation for others - it may be a compliment, a thank you note, or an acknowledgement of how they handled a particular situation. People don't get enough sincere appreciation and will remember you for it.

7. **Ask the same question twice.** This might sound counterintuitive because we think it shows we weren't listening. But in reality it can show we're active listening to all communication, verbal and non-verbal. One example is you ask someone "How are you?" and you get a short answer, "I'm good," but you sense that's not the case. If you ask again, "How are you - really?" chances are they may open up and begin an exchange.

8. **Ask for an introduction.** Be willing to ask for an introduction from someone if you feel a real connection has been made. Be careful not to overstep your bounds, especially if you haven't yet been able to offer a support exchange with that person. But many times people are willing to introduce you to someone in the initial stages of a Networlding relationship, because it's not a referral but simply a connection.

9. **Arrange another conversation.** Don't let your connection lose its momentum! Always follow-up on a great conversation by suggesting another meeting or conversation. Don't assume the other person will take the initiative.

SUPPLEMENT – SUPPORT EXCHANGE MODEL QUESTIONS AND EXPRESSIONS OF SUPPORT

FACILITATOR NOTE: This section is a supplement to this step in the Networlding process, and not something that needs to be taught. Point out to the class that these questions are there for them as support.

SCRIPT: An effective conversation with someone you are just meeting starts with questions that speak to the interests and needs of the person with whom you are speaking.

Finding out, first, what matters currently to someone you are talking with and second, working a conversation around what matters to them and to you, will grow a strong and lasting foundation for ongoing exchanges. There are questions and expressions for each stage of the model. As you practice weaving these questions and expressions into your conversations, add your own to the list!

CLOSING DISCUSSION: Ask for any additional questions, comments, or takeaways that the class has uncovered before moving on to step 5. You may also summarize the main points.

STEP 5 – GROW AND NURTURE RELATIONSHIPS

The fifth step in Networlding extends an initial exchange, with techniques to grow and nurture a relationship. The goal is to achieve even more dynamic and beneficial exchanges, moving along the Support Exchange Model.

For this segment, you may want a flip chart or whiteboard. Participants have a corresponding guide to follow along. Take time to familiarize yourself with the participant guide.

AGENDA

Customize the agenda timing as needed.

TIME	ACTION	OBJECTIVE
5 minutes	Introduction	Communicate overall objectives
5 minutes	**Exercise 1**: Exchange Circle	Extend new connections in group setting; demonstrate aspects of the exchange model
15 minutes	**Lesson 1**: Maximizing Networlding Interactions	Realize the value of regular interactions and provide specific steps
15-20 minutes	**Lesson 2**: Communicate on a More Meaningful level	Extending effective exchanges and meaningful relationships
20-30 minutes	**Exercise 2**: Meaningful Communication Role Play	Practice meaningful communication in a realistic role-play situation
N/A	**Supplement**: Networlding Exchange summary Tool	Point out that this tool is in their guides. It is a great way to help them document and capitalize on primary circle interactions.

OBJECTIVES

- Demonstrate and reinforce steps in the Support Exchange Model (through the Exchange Circle activity)
- Maximize our Networlding interactions
- Identify ways to improve communication skills so that exchanges are more meaningful
- Practice meaningful communication in a role-play situation

EXERCISE 1 – EXCHANGE CIRCLE (15 MINUTES)

SCRIPT: This activity is called the Exchange Circle. This models your Networlding circles and several steps within the exchange model. Plus we get to move around and hopefully meet some new potential Networlding partners!

FACILITATOR NOTE: For this activity, people will form a large circle. Depending on how many participants you have, decide whether to run this in one group or multiple. Ten people per group is about the max.

DIRECTIONS FOR FACILITATOR: First determine if you will run this activity in one or multiple circles. Time the activity, allowing 5-7 minutes.

1. Ask the group to assemble in a circle.

2. Within the circle, one person volunteers to come to the center.

3. The person in the center asks a question of the group that reflects something he/she enjoys doing, a place he/she has traveled, something about his/her business - the possibilities are endless. The goal is find common ground, as with a Networlding exchange. For example, "Who enjoys reading mystery novels?" or "Who is an entrepreneur?"

4. What happens next is like musical chairs. Each person in the circle (including the center person) that likes mystery novels is to move, finding a spot vacated by another mover who likes mystery novels. Let's say you have 4 movers in the outer circle, plus the center person. There will be one person left over who didn't get to a vacated spot quickly enough. That person now becomes the center person and asks a question of the group.

5. Repeat this process until each person (or as many as you have time for) has had the opportunity to be in the circle's center once.

6. Ask the class to return to their seats and proceed with the debrief.

DEBRIEF: Ask the class what they took away from this exercise.

Point out that Networlding partnerships require us to:

- Be open to learning more about others
- Step outside of our comfort zones
- Be curious and ask questions to find common ground
- Begin creating and then maintaining trust
- Be proactive

LESSON 1 – MAXIMIZE NETWORLDING INTERACTIONS (15 MINUTES)

SCRIPT: Let's quickly review the steps we've covered so far:

- In step 1, we created a values-based foundation from which to begin Networlding relationships

- In step 2, we created our primary circle - those 10 individuals with whom we share our closest connections and the possibilities to Networld

- In step 3, we took that a step further to expand our circles - learning the value of influencers, and creating our secondary and tertiary circles - and expanding our horizons of observability.

- In step 4, we became more familiar with the Support Exchange Model, and discussed the first four areas within that model: emotional, informational, knowledge, and promotional support. A Networlding relationship naturally follows the support exchange model, with the big goals of creating transformational opportunities and community.

Now in Step 5, we're going to discover how we grow and nurture those relationships. It's in growing and nurturing relationships - especially with our primary circle - that will make a difference in how successful we become at Networlding.

Growing your Networld is like growing a garden - it takes time, effort, care, and consistent action, It also takes mutual trust to create results. Before we talk about Networlding content, I'd like to get your input first.

SCRIPT (CLASS DISCUSSION):

- What have you done to successfully grow and nurture business relationships?
- How do you actively build mutual trust in your relationships?

FACILITATOR NOTE: Capture answers on a whiteboard or flipchart.

Capture answers on a whiteboard or flipchart. You may want to share any stories here, or ask the class for any examples.

66

SCRIPT: Great input everyone. Growing and nurturing relationships can be a challenging assignment because we feel often times as though we don't have enough time to dedicate to it. Ironically, we're more connected than ever via the Internet, but inside we often feel disconnected.

Networlding aspires to create a framework where we maximize our relationship-building time. We aren't frantically searching for contacts, but focusing on growing deeper relationships with the right people, people who are potential Networlding partners.

We've started this conversation with your ideas for growing and nurturing relationships. Let's continue by looking at some other ideas.

FACILITATOR NOTE: Be prepared with a story or two to illustrate and reinforce any of these points.

There is space within your participant guide to fill in the blanks.

1. **Schedule time for regular interactions.** Without a conscious time commitment (even if it's short) a budding relationship will fail to thrive. Ideally, set aside time on a monthly basis to share opportunities with your Networlding partnership. Find the ways to communicate that best fit your communication style and needs.

2. **Use the Networlding Exchange Summary** tool to keep your interactions on target and substantive. It can be very easy to get off track with our conversations - this will help keep the relationship growing in the right direction. You will see a sample of this tool in your participant guide as well.

3. **Develop a list of your top three things to accomplish.** Within each conversation, stick to 3 things you want to accomplish for that call. Limiting it to 3 will force you to be strategic and intentional, plus give you a great sense of accomplishment.

4. **Set expectations from the start and for each conversation.** When expectations aren't clearly articulated, and both sides aren't buying in, it can stall the relationship. For example, take a look at the goal you set back in step 1. If that's your primary focus in the next 6 months, be clear about that and see where your potential Networlding partner stands. Do they want to work on your opportunity, or do they have other expectations/opportunities to address?

5. **Brainstorm.** Idea creation is so important to the Networlding process, so take time during a conversation or in another method that works for you (email for example) and make sure you're keeping the flow of ideas going.

6. **Share connections.** Introducing and being introduced to others leads to gratitude and respect - which help your relationships blossom. Think
about a time someone introduced you to a great contact - how did you feel about the person who connected you? Ask these two questions of one another often: "Who do you know?" (open-ended) and "Do you know X?" (closed). Asking both increases the odds you'll cover all the people bases.

7. **Prepare for each conversation.** Preparation breeds confidence and shows your commitment to the Networlding partnership. Before each conversation, consider creating an agenda. Know what you want to share, what you want to accomplish and what information you need.

8. **Keep the discussions current.** Topical, timely exchanges fuel relationship growth. Don't focus on the past or old information - always strive to stay fresh. When you learn new information or make a new contact, make it a point to share quickly and often with your Networlding partners. This openness generates a greater number of quality opportunities.

9. **Overlap your circles.** Become highly aware of who is in your primary, secondary, and tertiary circles and share the names of these people with your Networlding partners (and vice versa). It's a sign of generosity and trust to open your circles to one another.

10. **Create action steps.** All talk and no action will lead you in circles rather than to a set goal. In each interaction, be sure to create at least one meaningful action step that each person will accomplish and commit to it. And in between conversations, lend support following the support exchange model. What emotional, information, knowledge, or promotional support can you offer each other to achieve your action steps?

11. **Summarize and set the next conversation.** This seems pretty obvious, but it's often overlooked. Summarize the key points from the exchange and determine when you will meet next. If you don't do this, it's easy to let the things of life get in the way and unintentionally stall the relationship and your goals.

SCRIPT: We've covered a lot of ideas here, between your contributions and the Networlding content. Are there any questions, comments, or experiences, you would like to share before we move on?

LESSON 2 – COMMUNICATE ON A MORE MEANINGFUL LEVEL (15-20 MINUTES)

SCRIPT: In lesson 1 we talked about some tactical ways to maximize your interactions with Networlding partners. In this lesson we're going to discuss the internal work of communicating on a more meaningful level with others. We will discuss:

1. Understanding communication styles
2. Active listening
3. Communication equality
4. Staying connected

Each action leads to enjoying equal opportunities in the relationship.

There is space in your participant guide to take notes and jot down ideas for your own Networlding partners.

Let's first talk about **communication styles(1)**.

We touched briefly on it in the previous step. Some people are talkers who enjoy pontificating; others are listeners who love to hear others speak. There are people who quickly get to a point and can't stand it when others don't do the same. Ideally you're aware of one other's styles and adapt accordingly.

Within communication styles, we have to pay attention to the other person's language and adopting it. This is also known as "mirroring," and that was discussed in step 4 as well. Mirroring helps facilitate consensus and understanding, shows we have sensitivity to others, and that we're listening carefully.

For example, does the other person:

- Have a very business-like style or does he or she use more colloquialism?
- Use a lot of industry jargon?
- Speak with brevity, or is he or she long-winded?
- String lots of sentences together without pausing for input?

Being aware of these styles and adapting to them - while still being you - will help you establish a better bond.

Next, let's talk about **active listening (2).**

Do you validate others by showing active, rather than passive, listening? In passive listening, you sit there and absorb, rather than respond. And the speaker may feel as though what he or she is saying is not impacting you - it may have a negative consequence.

On the other hand, if you're an active listener, you're truly trying to respond to and understand the other person. You're leaning forward, you're attentive. You might nod your head occasionally or ask a thoughtful question to show you're following along and really paying attention to the other person. You see the difference?

Then there is also the issue of **communication equality (3).** What this means, is there an equal sharing of:

- Ideas and information
- Talking and listening
- Questions and commentary

If you feel that the communication is one-sided, it can start to cause friction in the relationship, so it needs to be addressed right away. But it doesn't need to be perfect - we're all different and bring different skills to the table. There will be times when someone may contribute lots of ideas, or ask lots of questions . . . what you're looking for is overall equality.

Lastly, let's talk about how we **establish comfortable ways of staying connected (4).** For example, if you love to talk via phone, but your partner prefers email, you need to find some common ground. Make it a point to ask the people you're connecting with how they like to communicate, and make sure they know your preferred methods so you can decide together how best to accomplish it. It shows thoughtfulness and respect on your part.

So each of the four examples we just talked about - communication styles, active listening, communication equality, and staying connected - all improve our chances of enjoying equal-opportunity relationships.

Although opportunities may be difficult to come by in the initiating stage of Networld relationships, they become more plentiful as relationships evolve. You and your partner become more comfortable with one another and more willing to extend your trust. The biggest difference I hope you see is that opportunity development becomes *consciousand intentional*, rather than *unconscious and reactive*.

So, how do we enjoy equal opportunity relationships? There are fill-in-the-blanks in your guide and space for notes while we discuss.

FACILITATOR NOTE: Point out the fill-in-the-blanks to the class.

1. Identify the opportunities
2. Exchange wisdom support
3. Build community
4. Be proactive

Let's talk about **identifying opportunities(1)**. First, always know that opportunities surround you and your Networlding partners. The trick is to flush them out into the open. Keep your horizon of observability in mind - that even though connections and possibilities are not immediately visible, they are there.

SCRIPT (CLASS DISCUSSION): So how do you begin to identify new opportunities within your reach?

FACILITATOR: Capture ideas from the class on a whiteboard or flipchart. Be prepared to share a story of how you identified a Networlding opportunity.

SCRIPT: Great ideas everyone. Let's talk about some other potential ideas.

1. Has there been a hot topic of discussion between you and your partner or others?
2. Are there articles or blogs you've recently read?
3. What about discussions on social media sites, like LinkedIn and Twitter?
4. Is there a wished-for dream or opportunity that just doesn't seem to be there?

STORY EXAMPLE (INSERT YOUR OWN): I began telling you a story back in step 4 about the person I met at an industry group who is now part of my primary circle. We were at breakfast one day, talking about women in business and business skills - joking about how we wished we had some type of class in college that taught us all the stuff we really needed to know about starting out in the business world. Things like networking, knowing how to interact with co-workers and management, professional development, personal finance, etc.

Well that joking sparked an idea for a live workshop, aimed at millennial women to teach them those exact skills. From there we started brainstorming potential influential people to help us accomplish this, content ideas, presenters, etc. We're still in the exploring stages of that opportunity, but it started by talking a hot topic or a wished-for opportunity!

So the first point was about identifying opportunities. The **second point is exchanging wisdom support (2).** You'll remember from the support exchange model that wisdom support follows promotional support.

SCRIPT (CLASS DISCUSSION): Can anyone describe for me the difference between knowledge and wisdom?

FACILITATOR NOTE: Allow the class to discuss their perceived differences between knowledge and wisdom before sharing from Networlding.

SCRIPT: Great input everyone. Knowledge can be seen as knowing facts and sharing our experience with others. Wisdom takes knowledge further by adding good judgment, common sense, and sense of spirit to what we know. Wisdom not only helps us make enlightened decisions, but to help others see a situation from a different light and maybe make a better decision for themselves.

Offering wisdom support can be a much tougher, and definitely deeper, exchange with someone because it might involve having to say things that others may not want to hear.

Does anyone have a story they would like to share that shows the difference between knowledge and wisdom?

FACILITATOR NOTE: You may want to have an example or story of wisdom support to share with the class.

The next step in creating equal opportunities is to **build community (3)**. As we become more connected, what we share affects more people.

As you decide where you will place your energies in relationships, realize that you don't have to work as hard as you think to make a powerful difference for your Networld partners and the many lives you will impact as your opportunities expand. This is the ultimate effect of effective Networlding. And because we live in a world community, it's not unlikely that some of your Networlding partners will live around the globe.

The fourth step is to **be proactive (4)**. As we've already talked about, networkers tend to be more reactive and as Networlders, we have to be proactive in how we relate to our Networlding partners. Recognize that if you take the initiative and do more than your fair share, you'll not only increase your chances of getting opportunities, but you will spur others to action.

SCRIPT (CLASS DISCUSSION): What are some ways you can be proactive in your Networlding relationships when it comes to opportunities?

FACILITATOR NOTE: Allow the class to discuss before sharing from Networlding.

SCRIPT: Great input everyone. Here are some other ideas on being proactive:

1. Consider one of your Networlding partner's goals and create a list of people you know that might be able to help them and ask your partner if he/she would like the referrals.

2. Anticipate needs rather than waiting to be asked.

3. Mark down opportunities as they occur to you. It might be a job opening, a project, or connection.

4. Communicate potential opportunities regularly. They may not always turn into something, but just that simple communication shows that you're aware of what's important to your partners.

EXERCISE 2 – MEANINGFUL COMMUNICATION ROLE PLAY (15 MINUTES)

SCRIPT: In this lesson we talked about how meaningful communication and how it plays a critical role in growing and nurturing relationships, and identifying the right opportunities for Networlding partners.

In this activity, we're going to create a role play around meaningful communication, so you can prepare for it in real-life exchanges.

FACILITATOR NOTE: An example situation is provided, but you may alter it or add others based on your audience's situation. Both the directions and example situation are in the participant guide so they can follow along.

DIRECTIONS FOR FACILITATOR: Have the class divide into groups of 4-6 people. Read the following directions to the class.

1. Your group is going to read the example situation, and create a role play. The example is generic, so please draw on your own experiences and add your own insights and details to the situation.

2. The goal of your role play is to reflect the different meaningful communication elements we discussed in lesson 2. But, feel free to add elements from lesson 1 as you see fit. It's up to you whether you show the good side or the not-so-good side of communication.

3. We'll take the next 5-7 minutes to create the role play, and then we'll have each group present.

4. Have fun with this!

EXAMPLE SITUATION FOR ROLE PLAY: One of you (choose which person) has identified potential Networlding partners through various situations, such as a live networking event, LinkedIn, and a trusted referral source.

You've talked with each one several times individually and have exchanged emotional, informational, and knowledge support with them, so there is some level of trust.

You have a goal you would like to reach in the next year, and you've decided to bring these individuals together in an in-person meeting because you think they might be a good fit for your primary circle and to bring the opportunity to reality.

They know of one another through you, and there have been some basic email introductions, but overall you're all still in the initial support exchange stages.

Applying what you now know about creating more meaningful communication, design a short role play that shows:

- Communication styles
- Passive and active listening
- Communication equality
- Staying connected

You may also choose to incorporate elements of lesson 1 into your role play as well.

FACILITATOR NOTE: Once 5-7 minutes has passed, bring the class together and ask several groups to present their role play. In between each role play use the debrief script below.

Debrief (script): Great job everyone! In the role play:

- What meaningful communication did you observe?
- Was there any negative communication you observed?
- How did the group (or did the group) establish trust?
- Overall, do you think the exchange was maximized to its potential?
- What did you learn that you could apply to your real-life exchanges?

CLOSING DISCUSSION: Ask for any additional questions, comments, or takeaways that the class has uncovered before moving on to step 6. You may also summarize the main points.

SUPPLEMENT – NETWORLDING EXCHANGE SUMMARY TOOL

SCRIPT: This tool is in your participant guide. Use it to help you capitalize on interactions with your primary circle.

Networlding Partner	Meeting Information
Name:	Today's date/time:
Title:	Last meeting date/time:
Company Name:	Next meeting date/time:
Telephone:	
Website:	

Section 1: Referral Log of Names
(Name, Contact Information, Nature of Referral)

Section 2: Project Collaborations

Section 3: To Do (Prioritize)
1.
2.
3.
4.
5.

Section 4: "Who Do You Know" or "Do You Know"

STEP 6 – CO-CREATE OPPORTUNITIES

The sixth step in Networlding moves into opportunity creation. Creating opportunities together means that two Networlding partners expand their Networlding to new levels by leveraging their combined talent. Joint opportunities are more likely to occur as the relationship reaches maturity.

For this segment, you may want a flip chart or whiteboard. Participants have a corresponding guide to follow along. Take time to familiarize yourself with the participant guide.

AGENDA

Customize the agenda timing as needed.

TIME	ACTION	OBJECTIVE
5 minutes	Introduction	Communicate overall objectives
20 -30 minutes	**Lesson 1**: Co-Creation is the Networlding Way	Identify the ten guidelines for co-creating opportunities.
20 minutes	**Exercise 1**: Co-Creation in Action	Practice the guidelines for co-creation by brainstorming and on a participant's goal or idea.
15 minutes	**Lesson 2**:Behaviors for Co-Creation Success	Identify the opportunistic behaviors co-creation success.

OBJECTIVES

- Identify co-creation and its value to Networlding
- Discover ten guidelines for acting on joint opportunities
- Identify opportunistic behaviors in Networlding interactions

LESSON 1 – CO-CREATION IS THE NETWORLDING WAY (20-30 MINUTES)

SCRIPT: The Networlding process has hopefully helped you develop a deeper understanding of the value of quality relationships. When we choose the Networlding way to connect with others, those relationships enrich our lives and lead to transformational opportunities.

How can you best create transformational opportunities? Sometimes you're so focused on your day-to-day obligations that you fail to take the time to create, or co-create with your Networlding partners, opportunities that could benefit you and your organization in powerful, unique ways.

You can achieve your goals much faster if you use your Networlding partnerships as brain trusts. In addition, your partners can help you find things you didn't know existed, and enable you to avoid roadblocks and obstacles to success.

SCRIPT (CLASS DISCUSSION): Let's first talk about two terms, "co-create" and "transformational opportunity."

FACILITATOR NOTE: Capture answers on a whiteboard or flipchart.

- What does the term "co-create" mean to you?
- Now what does the term "transformational opportunity" mean to you?

SCRIPT: Great input everyone. Co-creating opportunities means that two Networlding partners expand their Networlding to new levels by leveraging their combined talent. As your relationships mature with your Networlding partners, co-creating becomes a natural extension of your relationships. Think of co-creating as moving from talk to action!

We don't initiate Networlding relationships just for the sake of it. At the heart of Networlding is the creation of transformational opportunities. These are opportunities that can truly change your career, your business, your community, or even your life. They speak to your heart rather than your head. You and your Networlding partners listen to one another; you understand what matters most, what stirs your passions - and as a result, expand that horizon of observability - creating opportunities beyond what you thought possible.

SCRIPT (CLASS DISCUSSION): We've probably all participated to some extent in co-creating an opportunity, even if we called it something else, or we weren't really aware of it at the time.

Think back to a successful opportunity you created with others are there any traits about the opportunity itself or the people involved that stood out to you?

FACILITATOR NOTE: Discuss this question as a class for a minute or two before moving on to the following guidelines.

SCRIPT: No matter how or where opportunities are co-created, the process remains relatively constant.

Let's look at the ten guidelines networlders use to find and act on these opportunities.

There is space in your participant guide to fill these in and take notes.

FACILITATOR NOTE: As you review these guidelines, ask the class for any stories or examples that illustrate them. Be prepared to share a story or two of your own.

1. **Analyze complementary strengths.** Creativity springs from our differences - not in values or goals, but in skills, knowledge, and experiences. You listed your top strengths way back in step 1. Sit down with your Networlding partner and get to know his or strengths. One thing to look out for - if you're both talented or skilled in the same areas this could be problematic as you co-create opportunities. Why? You could risk duplicating one another, or not pushing each other in new directions.
It's something to be aware of - you may need to bring in a third partner with a complementary strength.

2. **Share intentions.** This can be a tough one for people. Why? Because we sometimes operate from fear. Fear of sharing too much about ourselves; fear of people "stealing" our ideas; fear that someone will tear down their idea and rob them of the energy they need to make it happen.
Sharing our intentions is an act of faith; we have to trust that our Networlding partners will respond in kind - and that we are honest, constructive, and fair with one another. When you openly share your intentions, it sparks dialogue - it can enhance your idea and lead to other, better ideas.

3. **Articulate and analyze opportunities.** Networlders aren't shy about examining opportunities from all angles - this is how they co-create the best possible scenario. This involves a significant amount of openness, and a lack of defensiveness.

There are some key questions Networlders ask of one another to help improve the odds of coming up with a joint opportunity. Those questions are listed for you in your guide.

    a. What one opportunity do we hope to develop within the next 3 months?

    b. How does the opportunity reflect our values and strengths?

    c. How does it help us achieve our goals?

    d. What types of resources do we need to take full advantage of the opportunity?

    e. Who are all the people or organizations that could be involved with the opportunity?

    f. What first steps do we need to take to initiate the opportunity?

    g. Who else in our Networld might prove to be of assistance?

    h. What roadblocks might hamper this opportunity from developing; what creative solutions can we devise to address them?

4. **Practice reciprocity.** This might seem obvious, but reciprocity often becomes lost when an individual single-mindedly focuses on an opportunity. Without reciprocity, Networlding relationships collapse and resentment is created.

   There are times when an opportunity benefits each Networlding partner equally, and reciprocity is a given. But there will also be times when one person may benefit more than the other from an opportunity. In those cases, the one experiencing greater benefit needs to make every effort to help the other with a project in the future. Examine cross-selling possibilities.

5. **Examine cross-selling possibilities.** An opportunity isn't simply a present "deal" between two partners; Networlders look to extend an opportunity to others. This isn't natural for most people. A hoarding mentality - based on a fear that someone will get more than we are getting - is common. When it comes to sharing clients and referrals, it can generate a lot of negative emotions. Networlders recognize this fear and make every attempt to openly discuss that issue.

6. **Form strategic alliances.** Who should you partner with? Should you be purely opportunistic and partner with the person who is in the best position to develop a specific opportunity? Does it matter if the person is in your primary, secondary, or tertiary circle?

As a general rule of thumb, it makes sense to concentrate on co-creating with people in your primary circle. They're the ones who have the influence and shared values you need to produce a positive collaborative effort. But realize that not everyone in your primary circle will lead you to the types of opportunities you're looking for at a given time in your life.

One person may help you achieve specific goals better than another - this is why you want to create strategic alliances. These are relationships you form to focus on targeted opportunities. They are strategic in the sense that they're planned - with long-term and short-term goals in mind, as well as the resources, tactics, and other elements needed.

Here are some questions to help you determine if co-creating with a given person will result in a strategic alliance. These questions are also in your guide:

    a. Does the person share your goals in creating opportunities? What is motivating the other person, and does this match your motivation?

    b. Are the other person's strengths complementary or redundant to your own? Are they relevant to the type of opportunity you're pursuing?

    c. Does your prospective co-creator have the influence necessary to help you achieve your opportunity objectives, and is that person willing to use his/her influence?

    d. If this individual won't benefit as much as you will from this opportunity, are you in a position to help her achieve her goals for opportunities that are more beneficial to her?

    e. If you look at your Networld and your prospective co-creator's Networld, is there enough reach to the people and resources necessary to achieve your opportunity goals?

7. **Create mentoring opportunities.** Networlders create opportunities in all sorts of ways, and one very important way is mentoring. Think of the people who have mentored you in your endeavors, many times for no financial gain, just the reward of helping you and learning from you. Networlders know the value of mentoring and realize its value is a two-way street. Consider how you can incorporate mentoring in your opportunity creation, formal or informal.

8. **Bridge divergent Networlds.** Co-creating also means constantly locating new people with similar values from diverse backgrounds. This allows you access to more diverse opportunities. People tend to run in redundant circles, so what happens is they continue to connect with the same people over long periods of time, and sometimes never venturing beyond those connections. Bridging divergent Networlds is a conscious effort; it's one you have to make in order to expand your horizon of observability.

FACILITATOR NOTE: You may ask the class for their ideas on ways to bridge Networlds before giving them these ideas. These ideas are in your participant guide as well.

    a. Join clubs, associations, or other groups that are organized not by profession but by some interest that encourages diversity; think civic organizations, political committees, not-for-profit volunteer groups, etc.

    b. Ask others in your Networld if you can go with them to a meeting, seminar, or conference where the people are from different professions, have different interests, or different ethnicity/culture from you.

    c. Connect with family/friends who might provide you with an introduction to people who are significantly different from the people you typically associate with.

    d. Use joint opportunities created with a Networlding partner as "recruiting" tools to bring in people with divergent skills and knowledge in pursuit of your common goal.

9. **Play with opportunities.** Rather than look at things in a businesslike and linear approach, be more adventurous! Don't ignore obvious opportunities at your fingertips, but always be aware for what's beyond the opportunity in front of you.

FACILITATOR NOTE: You might ask the class in what ways they've played and explored ideas before sharing these ideas. These ideas are in your participant guide as well:

    a. Create variations on your idea theme. See how many different ways you can spin your idea - you'll be surprised with what you come up with!

b. Identify someone else's opportunity to see how you might contribute. What are those in your Networlding circles doing where your knowledge and skills might help their project flourish?

c. Use provocative, unexpected questions to push opportunities further. Ask, and then ask more. We're very quick to want or provide answers, and very slow to ask. The more questions you ask, the more creative you can be in discovering opportunities.

10. **Think peripherally.** This is a figurative "turning of the head." Our focus can become so singular that we don't see what's in our peripheral vision. We all have blind spots to opportunities. How do you solve that? Make it a habit to look beyond your daily routines, get out of your comfort zone. Divergent Networlds facilitate this because you are constantly exposed to new people and ideas.

How can you adapt your interests, skills and knowledge, a product, or a service into a seemingly unrelated use?

EXERCISE 1 – CO-CREATION IN ACTION (25-30 MINUTES)

SCRIPT: This is your opportunity to begin co-creation, right here, today.

You'll be putting your new knowledge of values, circle partners, the support exchange model, and relationship exchanges into practice.

DIRECTIONS FOR FACILITATOR: This activity can be done in table groups of 4-6 people. Allow 20 minutes for the activity; adapt this time as necessary for your needs.

Explain the following directions to the class:

1. You'll work at your tables in small groups (about 4-6 people).

2. Select one person from your table who would like their goal or idea to be the brainstorm subject for co-creation opportunities.

3. Use as many of the ten guidelines as possible that apply to the goal or idea being discussed. Be adventurous and playful! When you use the principles of Networlding you can't go wrong.

   Other questions to consider:

   - Who in your primary circle may be a possible Networlding partner?

   - Who else in your Networld may be able to contribute to the idea's success?

   - How can you start exchanges with your Networlding partner(s)?

   - What obstacles do you see stopping you? And how can you overcome them?

   - How will bringing this opportunity to fruition be transformational?

4. The end result is hopefully an expansion on the idea or goal in question, possible co-creation opportunities, and some next steps toward making it a reality.

DEBRIEF: At the 20-minute mark, bring the class back together. Allow 5-10 minutes for discussion. Select one table (or as many as time permits) to share what they discussed. Use the following questions to encourage discussion:

- How did the guidelines influence your discussion?

- What next steps can the person take (who shared their idea for the activity) to further their idea or goal?

- How is the Networlding co-creation process different from how you've approached opportunities in the past?

- How can this process help you going forward?

LESSON 2 – BEHAVIORS FOR CO-CREATION SUCCESS (15 MINUTES)

SCRIPT: The ten guidelines we just learned facilitate the co-creation process. You're probably realizing that because each opportunity is unique, some guidelines may be used more in depth than others.

But there are some behaviors that apply to every co-creation opportunity. Practicing these behaviors will make a difference in the quantity and quality of your co-creation possibilities. Essentially this means saying and doing things that encourage others to co-create with you or lend support to the opportunities that you're targeting.

Here's a checklist for you. There are fill-in-the-blanks in your participant guide to follow along:

1. **Continuously share information about your abilities.** This isn't bragging or being self-centered, it's simply making your Network aware of your skills and knowledge. They'll appreciate knowing this information when they have an opportunity or goal.

2. **Treat your primary circle partners the same way as prospects.** Be willing to share opportunities with your primary circle partner. Treat them as if they were your best prospects by communicating regularly, being respectful and honest.

3. **Ask for and capitalize on referrals from your primary circle partners.** Never underestimate your circle's ability to provide referrals - and also be willing to provide them as well. If there's an opportunity you want to create, invite your primary circle to participate in its creation and development.

4. **Assess the influence of your primary circle members with referrals.** When you're provided with a referral, take time find out the relationship between your circle partner and referral to gauge the influence factor. The higher the influence factor, the less work you will likely have to do in making the interaction one that will facilitate your opportunity.

5. **Meet and exceed the opportunity needs of your primary circle partners.** Be proactive; volunteer information and ideas when people in your Networld send out a call for assistance. If you meet your partners' needs, they will be much more willing to meet yours.

6. **Demonstrate energy and commitment.** Networlding requires energy and it demands continuous communication. Co-creating opportunities is something that high-energy people do. Keep your commitments once you make them; magic happens when a committed Networld co-creates opportunities!

CLOSING DISCUSSION: Ask for any additional questions, comments, or takeaways that the class has uncovered before moving on to step 7. You may also summarize the main points.

STEP 7 – RE-CREATE YOUR NETWORLD

Networlds, and the relationships they hold, are dynamic rather that static. The seventh step is not the end of Networlding, but continuous monitoring, assessment, and reformulation of your Networld.

For this segment, you may want a flip chart or whiteboard. Participants have a corresponding guide to follow along. Take time to familiarize yourself with the participant guide.

AGENDA

Customize the agenda timing as needed.

Time	Action	OBJECTIVE
5 minutes	Introduction	Communicate overall objectives
30 minutes	**Lesson 1:** A Checklist for Your Networld	Tools to manage a fluid Networld for maximum efficiency and results
15 minutes	**Exercise 1:** Your Action Plan	Create an actionable plan to help learners apply this new information right away in their relationships
20 minutes	**Exercise 2:** Your Commitment to the Process	Table conversation and personal action plan to keep the process moving forward

OBJECTIVES

- Discover key ways to monitor, reassess, and reformulate your Networld for maximum impact - for you, your connections, and your community
- Create your commitment to the process

LESSON 1 – A CHECKLIST FOR YOUR NETWORLD (30 MINUTES)

SCRIPT: I'd like for you to picture your Networlding circles for a moment. Think about your primary, secondary, and tertiary circles. Your circles are fluid - people are moving in and out of those circles as you create connections and opportunities. As you grow and change, so will your circles. It's a natural and important part of Networlding - your Networld is never static, always moving.

SCRIPT (CLASS DISCUSSION): Let's talk about some examples first.

- Can anyone share a story or example of a networking relationship that has changed?

FACILITATOR NOTE: Ask them to share why they think it changed and what they learned from the experience (this will tie into the checklist). Also, be prepared with a story of your own, especially if participants are having a difficult time coming up with one.

SCRIPT: Great input everyone. It's important to remember that relationships do change over time. People will move in and out of our circles. As Networlders, we need to remain aware of that and open to new connection and new opportunities.

With that in mind, this seventh step is about keeping on top of developments in your Networld and using this awareness to re-create it as needed - and your place in it.

FACILITATOR NOTE: Be prepared with a story or two for some of these checklist points, or ask the class to share as you review them.

Keep this checklist top of mind when evaluating your Networld. This checklist is also in your participant guide.

1. **Reassess your goals, mission, and values.** Remember the house - you did this way back in step 1. But a lot of people don't take the time to do this, and it affects the quality of their relationships and results they achieve. There isn't a secret to knowing when a goal has stopped functioning for you, but it's a matter of measuring your passion for it.

   The same is true for your mission and values - tune into your instincts. Also, be sure you're talking to those in your primary circle about your goals, mission, and values - and theirs as well.

2. **Take the test of time.** One of the simplest and easiest ways to evaluate your Networld is to analyze how you're spending your time when you're in it. For example, are you spending 80% of your time
with 4 or 5 primary circle partners and creating mutual opportunities? Or are you spending that time with only 1-2 partners? If the latter is true, you need to re-create your Networld, rather than co-create opportunities.

3. **Monitor and maintain the exchange dynamic.** To do this, keep three things in mind.
   - First, keep in touch by communicating with your primary circle at least once a month. Be proactive! Don't wait for someone else to initiate the contact.

   - Second, design a strategy (or several) to keep the exchanges evolving and meaningful. For example, create a short agenda of key items or questions - to keep your communication on target and mutually beneficial.

   - Lastly, evaluate what was exchanged. Were both of you satisfied with the exchange? Did anything fall short? Being honest about this will continually improve the quality of your exchanges.

4. **Establish a comfortable work-life balance.** What happens when you become an established Networlder? You will have to deal with too many opportunities coming your way. It's easy to want to say yes to all of them, but part of the re-creating process is learning which opportunities to turn down. Evaluate each opportunity that presents itself in terms of your goals and values. Learn to say no (and this might be a process for you!) to those that don't fit. Keep this in mind: "You can tell the sign of a successful person by the number of times he or she can say no." It can be awkward at first . . . but you'll find with practice that you can do so gracefully and honestly - and you'll be respected for that.

5. **Continuously extend the connections.** It's easy to become comfortable with our immediate Networlding partners, but you always want to be looking to extend beyond that horizon of observability we've talked about. Two great questions to ask of your Networlding partners:

   - Who have you enjoyed working with?
   - And why?That first question helps you to identify individuals you could be introduced to (or introduce your partners to) and the second question helps match your interests, values, and goals that others may connect with. The key point here is to always remember there are so many connections beyond the obvious.

6. **Be open to new types of opportunities.** It's easy to fall into an opportunity rut! That means we keep pursuing the same types of opportunities, instead of new challenges. But, there is a tradeoff that takes place - with every opportunity you choose, another will be tabled, permanently or temporarily. So what do you do? Make sure your goals, mission, and values are clear - they will guide you to the right opportunities. Be intensely aware of what it is you really want to achieve in your life. Those choices become easier to make.

7. **Keep a maintenance checklist.** The best Networlders know that they can't coast when they get to step 7! To keep things fresh and effective, your Networld needs a tune up every once in awhile. Use this easy maintenance checklist:

   - Once a month, list out your exchanges. Compare it to the Support Exchange model and determine those exchanges are helping you meet your goals.

   - Are your primary circle partners also your friends? Networlding isn't all business, so if you're partner are not friends, that's a sign something is wrong.

   - Evaluate your primary and secondary circles once a quarter. Ask yourself, "Should this person remain in that circle?" Your Networld is fluid, so don't be afraid to move people in and out of those circles.

   - Are your Networlding partners satisfied with the support and opportunities you're giving them? Encourage your partners to be honest with you about their satisfaction with the relationship - because if they aren't, you're likely to see less and less support on their part.

8. **Position (or reposition) yourself as a resource.** Don't assume that everyone knows what you have to offer. People often forget (or are unaware) of your talents and skills. With that in mind, graciously keep your primary circle members up-to-date on your projects and professional development opportunities. The Networlders who receive the most opportunities are those that regularly communicate and are known as resource providers.

9. **Be ambitious about Networlding.** Here's a quick activity for you: jot down 3-5 influential people in your industry that you would like to meet.

FACILITATOR NOTE: Allow a minute or two for this.
Now that you've done that, communicate that list to everyone in your primary circle. Now you may not get a direct connection right away, but putting it out there lets others know, and that awareness can eventually begin to generate a pathway to a connection.

10. **Know when a relationship should end.** This one can be particularly difficult because we don't want to hurt feelings or burn bridges. But there will be times when relationships will need to end, for whatever the reason. There isn't a formula to follow, but be aware of a few things:

   - Have you or your partner shifted goals? This makes it very difficult to create joint opportunities.
   - Did your partner's values change (or possibly come to light)? You may discover you don't share the same values - what's important to you isn't as important to your partner as you initially thought.

   - Is there a lack of reciprocity? You discover your partner is more of a taker, rather than an exchanger and this creates an issue.

Listen to your instincts! And be honest and sensitive when you discuss this with your partner. It may be an issue that can be cleared up quickly, or it could be something deeper. Focus on the positives, do your best to not dwell on the negatives and create a rift. Also, remain open to a future reconnection!

11. **Develop Networlding savvy and maturity.** This will come with time and practice, but there are few techniques that can help accelerate your savvy and maturity in the process:

   - <u>Provide post-referral feedback</u>. When someone makes a referral for you, be sure to let them know the results. It shows your appreciation for the other person's efforts, and increases your odds of obtaining future referrals.

   - <u>Don't push a relationship</u>. There's a difference between proactive and assertive . . . and pushy. Networlders aren't pushy. For example, it's not pushy to ask for a referral; it is pushy to ask over and over again. Put yourself in your partner's shoes, read their body language, or gauge their tone of voice. You'll see the difference in how people become more open to you.

- Keep confidences. When you are known as someone who is reliable and able to keep something in confidence, you will become a magnet for information! As you re-create your Networld, information is your most valuable asset.

- Learn to delegate. As you build stronger and stronger Networlds, the demands on your time will increase. You will have to prioritize what you will do and what to delegate.

- Slow down to speed up. We move at the speed of light sometimes, and our relationships can suffer for it. A savvy, mature Networlder take a deep breath and reflects before moving forward on a connection or opportunity. Choose carefully, and you increase the odds of choosing correctly! This process may take you a bit longer, but you will be rewarded with reaching your destination that much faster because you chose correctly the first time.

- Repair relationships. Point #10 talks about ending relationships. But a savvy and mature Networlder never does this prematurely. Recreating your Networld makes waves, and sometimes people aren't ready for those waves. So, when a rift does occur, use it as an opportunity for open, honest communication. Attempt to repair any breaks in the relationships where it makes sense.

EXERCISE 1 - YOUR ACTION PLAN (15 MINUTES)

SCRIPT: This is one of your last activities in the Networlding course, your action plan! The goal is to help you keep the momentum going and the learning fresh - so you can create your Networld once you leave here.

Ideally, you should fill this out once a month for consistency and results. There is an action plan in your student guide.

DIRECTIONS FOR FACILITATOR: Ask the class to take the next 10-12 minutes (individually) to begin filling in their action plan. They won't complete it in the allotted time, but the idea is get them started so they can finish on their own.

On the following pages is a copy of the action plan they will see in their guide.

DEBRIEF: At the 10-12 minute mark, ask the participants to wrap up their action plan and remind them to complete them on their own. Make the following points about the action plan:

1. It is designed to be incorporated on a monthly basis so you can track your progress and relationship building.

2. You can also see at a high level where you need to make improvements, and the positive impact you're having by co-creating opportunities with the right people in the right way.

3. It works best when your primary circle partners use it as well!

SUPPLEMENT - YOUR ACTION PLAN

Month: What are the results I have achieved to date on my goal? Changes to goal (if applicable): What top benefits have I received from my primary circle partners this month? What top benefits have I offered my primary circle partners this month?	

Partners supported:	What did I give? What did I receive?
Great organizations or trade shows I have attended:	Details of the event and top people to follow up with:

Organizations I plan to join:	Special committees, events, or people to connect with:
Great referrals I have received:	Contact details, context of referral, and conversation starter suggestions
Great potential primary circle partners:	Scheduled meetings and conversations I will initiate:
Partners I will follow up with in the next month:	Ideas for support I can offer, ideas for support I can request:

Partners I plan to co-create opportunities with in the next month:	Ideas and details:
Top partnering story:	
Overall estimated financial results from connections:	Breakdown of results:
To do's:	Details:

EXERCISE 2 - YOUR COMMITMENT TO THE NETWORLDING PROCESS (20 MINUTES)

SCRIPT: In this final activity, you'll have the chance to review your learning from the previous steps. Networlding works best when you add the best practices you've learned here to your collective knowledge base. And when you actively practice, you retain more information and hopefully utilize it in your daily interactions.

DIRECTIONS FOR FACILITATOR: This is a discussion activity to be conducted at each table. There is space in the participant guide for notes. Allow 10-12 minutes for discussion.

Explain the following directions to the class:

1. You'll work at your tables.

2. Discuss the following questions at your table.

   - What are 2 key lessons you've learned in this process that will help you become a better Networlder?

   - What new opportunities (or potential opportunities) have you either identified or created as a result of this course? These opportunities could be professional or personal.

   - What support can you provide your Networlding partners to help them achieve their goals, and what further support can you ask for in achieving your goals?

DEBRIEF: At the 12-minute mark, bring the class back together. Allow the next 8 minutes for discussion. Ask for volunteers to share these two pieces of information:

- What key lessons have you learned to help you become a better Networlder?

- What new opportunities have you either identified or created as a result of this course?

FACILITATOR NOTE: You may wish to close with a final review of each of the steps in the Networlding process. Encourage the class to support one another in the Networlding process - you may even find they are doing this already!

SCRIPT: Excellent job everyone! As you'll learn, the real payoff for working and living in the Networlding universe goes far beyond the many opportunities you create with others.

The process gives you the chance to be successful and the chance to help others become successful. When you interact with people as a true Networlder, you not only reap professional rewards but also understand that you've made the world a better place for both the people you know and people in need.

CLOSING DISCUSSION: Ask for any additional questions, comments, or takeaways that the class has uncovered. You may also summarize the seven steps of Networlding again.